THE STATE OF THE WORLD'S CHILDREN
1997

Oxford University Press, Walton Street,
Oxford, OX2 6DP, Oxfordshire, UK.
Oxford, New York, Toronto, Delhi, Bombay,
Calcutta, Madras, Karachi, Kuala Lumpur,
Singapore, Hong Kong, Tokyo, Nairobi,
Dar-es-Salaam, Cape Town, Melbourne,
Auckland and associated companies in
Berlin and Ibadan.

Oxford is a trade mark of Oxford
University Press.
Published in the United States by
Oxford University Press, New York.

British Library Cataloguing in
Publication Data
The state of the world's children 1997
1. Children—Care and hygiene
613'0432 RJ101

ISBN 0-19-262871-2
ISSN 0265-718X

The Library of Congress has catalogued this
serial publication as follows:
The state of the world's children—Oxford and
New York: Oxford University Press
for UNICEF
v.; ill.; 20cm. Annual. Began publication
in 1980.
1. Children—Developing countries—
Periodicals.
2. Children—Care and hygiene—Developing
countries—Periodicals. I. UNICEF.
HQ 792.2. S73 83-647550 362.7' 1'091724

UNICEF, UNICEF House, 3 UN Plaza,
New York, NY 10017, USA.

UNICEF, Palais des Nations, CH-1211,
Geneva 10, Switzerland.

Cover photo
Honduras, 1989, UNICEF/89-0052/Vauclair

Back cover photo
Cambodia, 1992, UNICEF/92-5895/Lemoyne

THE STATE OF THE WORLD'S CHILDREN 1997

Carol Bellamy, Executive Director,
United Nations Children's Fund

United Nations Children's Fund

Published for UNICEF by

Oxford University Press

Contents

The Convention on the Rights of the Child is at the core of a revolutionary shift in the world's approach to children. The idea that children have special needs, which sparked the founding of UNICEF 50 years ago, has now given way to the conviction that children have the same spectrum of rights as adults: civil and political, social, cultural and economic. The Convention, nearing universal ratification, is setting in motion profound changes in laws, policies, institutions and practices. UNICEF itself has adopted a mission statement that looks to the Convention as its guiding force.

This chapter shows how the world's course towards peace, equality, development and justice can be hastened and helped by the energies the Convention is generating. The year 2000 goals, established at the World Summit for Children in 1990, must now be pursued in the context of the Convention. Progress towards those goals, according to a report in late 1996 by the UN Secretary-General, shows great strides made, with millions of children's lives saved since 1990. But much remains to be done. The Convention expands the scope of action now under way and calls for continuing commitments of both political will and resources.

Over 250 million children around the world — in countries rich and poor — work and many of them are at risk from hazardous and exploitative labour. Denied education and trapped in cycles of poverty, their most basic rights, their health and even their lives are in jeopardy. This chapter examines the issue of child labour in all its complexity, exposing the common myths about it and exploring the causes. The contributing factors are multiple and overlapping, including the exploitation of poverty, lack of access to education, and traditional restrictions, particularly for girls. Compounding the problem is the paucity of statistics about the number of children working, especially those in hazardous conditions. More data are urgently needed in order to better monitor and prevent child labour violations, particularly since the vast majority of children labour in invisibility.

Because the causes of child labour are complex, the solution must be comprehensive. The report calls for the immediate end to hazardous child labour and proposes strategies to help eliminate and prevent it including: access to education; wider legal protection; birth registration for all children; collection of information; and mobilization of the widest possible coalition of partners among governments, communities, non-governmental organizations (NGOs), employers and trade unions. The single most effective way to protect children from hazardous and exploitative labour, the report argues, is to extend and improve education so that it will attract them and inspire their lives.

Chapter III
Statistical tables

Statistics provide an essential foundation for gauging children's well-being and the level of care, nurture and resources they receive. Statistics such as those on child mortality, immunization, maternal mortality, malnutrition and school enrolment chart countries' progress towards achieving the goals set at the 1990 World Summit for Children. Despite significant gains, more than 12 million children under five still die each year, mainly from preventable diseases and malnutrition. The tables cover basic indicators, health, nutrition, education, demographics, economic progress and the situation of women, plus indicators on less populous countries, rates of progress and regional summaries. Countries are listed in descending order of their estimated 1995 under-five mortality rates, the first basic indicator in table 1.

77

Panels

Text figures

Foreword

The well-being of children has been the inspiration and the driving purpose of the United Nations Children's Fund for 50 years. It is from this unique perspective and experience that UNICEF adds its voice, concern and expertise to the debate about child labour, the primary focus of *The State of the World's Children 1997* report.

Child labour is a controversial and emotional issue. It is also a complex and challenging one that defies simple solutions. The thoughtful and comprehensive approaches required must be guided by the best interests of the child and by a commitment to children's human rights, as enshrined in the Convention on the Rights of the Child.

In this report, UNICEF urges that priority be given to efforts for the immediate end of hazardous and exploitative child labour and to urgent support for education, so that children may acquire the knowledge and skills that can enable them to improve their lives. It also stresses the need for basic services, social development strategies, income-generation measures and legal protection for children, their families and communities.

The United Nations and its related agencies have a long history of collaborative action on challenging questions concerning human development and human rights, the environment and global health. It is a record of which the world can be justly proud.

The State of the World's Children emphasizes the need for such collective action to deal with child labour. By working together, as the report makes clear, governments, international and national organizations and all members of the world community can help protect children from the economic exploitation so graphically described in this report. Ending hazardous child labour, a priority concern of the International Labour Organization and of UNICEF, now needs to become the world's shared and urgent goal. The United Nations system must take the lead.

Boutros Boutros-Ghali
United Nations Secretary-General

Chapter I

The Convention
on the Rights of the Child

A girl in a non-formal school programme run by community volunteers in Pakistan.

A new era for children

Fifty years ago, in the aftermath of the most devastating war in history, UNICEF was created on 11 December 1946 to provide succour to children. Its establishment stemmed from the concern that children would not be adequately protected in the overall relief effort under way in Europe. The international recognition that children required special attention was revolutionary at the time.

At the end of the postwar reconstruction period, developing countries emerging from the colonial era invoked the same principle to demand that children be given specific attention in international cooperation. UNICEF's initial relief mandate was enlarged to include the survival and development of children.

Now, the international approach to children has changed dramatically once again. The idea that children have special needs has given way to the conviction that children have rights, the same full spectrum of rights as adults: civil and political, social, cultural and economic.

This conviction, expressed as the Convention on the Rights of the Child, entered into international law on 2 September 1990, nine months after the Convention's adoption by the United Nations General Assembly. Since then, the Convention has been ratified (as of mid-September 1996) by all countries except the Cook Islands, Oman, Somalia, Switzerland, the United Arab Emirates and the United States, making it the most widely ratified human rights treaty in history.

The Convention has produced a profound change that is already beginning to have substantive effects on the world's attitude towards its children. Once a country ratifies, it is obliged in law to undertake all appropriate measures to assist parents and other responsible parties in fulfilling their obligations to children under the Convention. Now, 96 per cent of the world's children live in States that are legally obligated to protect children's rights.

Those rights are comprehensive. The Convention defines children as people below the age of 18 (article 1) whose "best interests" must be taken into account in all situations (article 3). It protects children's right to survive and develop (article 6) to their full potential, and among its provisions are those affirming children's right to the highest attainable standard of health care (article 24), and to express views (article 12) and receive information (article 13). Children have a right to be registered immedi-

The idea that children have special needs has given way to the conviction that children have rights, the same full spectrum of rights as adults: civil and political, social, cultural and economic.

A young girl in Beirut.

Children's rights, children's voices

"We need more bridges over the road so we can get to the park," says an eight-year-old from Bristol (United Kingdom). Across the Irish Sea, a seven-year-old says: "You need a see-saw and you need a big aeroplane and you need a wee rubber duck for your bath. You need somewhere to play."

Reports to the Committee on the Rights of the Child by States that have ratified the Convention are the vital centre-pieces of the monitoring process. However carefully and completely they may be done, nevertheless, official reports can rarely capture the fullest picture of children's rights in a given country. That is ideally drawn from a variety of sources and voices.

Alternative reports are important complements to official reports, providing depth, details and perspective. The words quoted above come from the *UK Agenda for Children*, produced by the Children's Rights Development Unit, a small British organization supported by the Gulbenkian Foundation and the UK Committee for UNICEF. Conceived as an alternative report and issued in July 1994, the *Agenda* has earned wide praise for its immediacy, relevance and comprehensiveness.

It manages to be thorough and substantive, as lively as a personal diary, as pertinent as a morning's headline and as urgent as a cry for help. Committee member Hoda Badran has called the *Agenda* "a major innovatory contribution" to the methodology of monitoring child rights in an individual country.

The innovations are several. The document is the culmination of two years of research on the part of the Unit and some 183 non-governmental organizations (NGOs) in England, Scotland, Wales and Northern Ireland. Such broad participation allows the report not only to review the UK's legislation and administrative procedures for compli-ance with the Convention, but also to examine what is actually happening in practice.

Moreover, it includes the input of children, another innovation that illustrates the extent to which the Unit and participating NGOs were inspired by the Convention's directives to let the views of children be heard and make the Convention provisions widely known to adults and children alike.

The voices of children echo throughout: "Parents shouldn't have the right to hit children," says a 13-year-old from Lincolnshire. "It just makes children grow up to be violent."

"At the age of 13, I was looking after the house, looking after my mum, shielding my mum from attacks from my dad — which is a hell of a lot for a 13-year-old to take on," says a 17-year-old from Merseyside.

"Kids can't play where I live; needles everywhere, stolen cars, no one cares," laments a 14-year-old from Manchester. School club members, children in jail, those in institutions, the homeless, those caring for sick or disabled parents, abused children and others were all heard in an effort to reflect the wide and often difficult realities of children's lives. The Unit set up more than 40 consultation sessions with children, who ranged in age from 6 to 18 years.

Their words strengthen the study, which analyses the Convention's articles grouped in 12 key policy areas: personal freedoms; care of children; physical and personal integrity; an adequate standard of living; health and health care services; environment; education; play and leisure; youth justice; child labour; immigration and nationality; children and violent conflict (Northern Ireland); abduction; and international obligations. Within each area, the UK's compliance with all relevant articles is examined, along with compliance with three general principles or 'umbrella' articles: non-discrimination (article 2), the best interests of the child (article 3) and the right of children to express views and have them taken seriously in all decisions affecting them (article 12).

Thus, an 18-year-old from Northern Ireland, quoted in the chapter on the "adequate standard of living" policy area, makes the impact of changes in the social security system come alive: "We have to lock the door, turn off the lights and pretend we are not in every time we see the rent man or the milkman."

Such contributions help bring to life an exhaustive study of children's rights for which no issue is too small for attention — school uniforms, the opening of mail in children's homes — or too large — for instance, the chapter on children and violent conflict, which is devoted exclusively to Northern Ireland. Transport policy, housing codes, environmental regulations are all put under the microscope.

Nor does any problem defy solution. Sections on Actions Required for Compliance appear within chapters, and the suggestions made are summarized at each chapter end. The Committee on the Rights of the Child could hardly have a clearer picture of the status of children's rights in the UK, nor a more systematic, constructive and eloquent guide to what needs to be done.

ately after birth and to have a name and nationality (article 7), a right to play (article 31) and to protection from all forms of sexual exploitation and sexual abuse (article 34).

The Convention recognizes that not all governments have the resources necessary to ensure all economic, social and cultural rights immediately. But it commits them to make those rights a priority and to ensure them to the maximum extent of available resources.

Fulfilling their obligations sometimes requires States to make fundamental changes in national laws, institutions, plans, policies and practices to bring them into line with the principles of the Convention.

The first priority must be to generate the political will to do this. As the drafters of the Convention recognized, real change in the lives of children will come about only when social attitudes and ethics progressively change to conform with laws and principles. And when, as actors in the process, children themselves know enough about their rights to claim them.

The official monitor of this process of change is the Committee on the Rights of the Child. Governments are obliged to report to the Committee within two years of ratification, and every five years thereafter, specifying the steps taken to change national laws and formulate policies and actions.

The Committee, made up of 10 experts, gathers evidence from non-governmental organizations (NGOs) and intergovernmental organizations, including UNICEF, and these groups may prepare alternative reports to that of a government (Panel 1). The Committee and the government then meet to discuss the country's child rights efforts and the steps necessary to overcome difficulties.

The reporting process has proved dynamic and constructive, with the dialogue established helping to advance children's rights. Unfortunately, however, many countries have missed their reporting deadlines, 28 of them by as much as three years, as of September 1996.

The process of implementing the Convention still remains in its infancy but, as we have noted, the international treaty for children is already beginning to make an impact. As reported in 1996 in UNICEF's annual publication, *The Progress of Nations,* of the 43 countries whose reports had been reviewed at the time, 14 had incorporated the principles of the Convention into their constitutions and 35 had passed new laws or amended existing laws to conform to the Convention. And 13 had built the Convention into curricula or courses to begin the key process of educating children about their rights.[1]

Around the world, teachers, lawyers, police officials, judges and caregivers are being trained in the principles and the application of the Convention. Inspired by the Convention, Sierra Leone has demobilized child soldiers. In Rwanda, UNICEF, under the Convention's aegis, has been working to move children held in adult detention centres for alleged war offences to special juvenile institutions and has hired lawyers to defend them. And reforms, changes and improvements continue to accumulate around the world (Panel 2).

The monitoring of the Convention and media coverage of the issues have promoted international awareness of gross violations of children's rights. Major initiatives such as the World Congress against Commercial Sexual Exploitation of Children, held in Stockholm in August 1996, and the International Conference on Child

UNICEF/3703/Rotner

Among the rights guaranteed by the Convention on the Rights of the Child is the right to play. A boy on a rope-swing in Barbados, where the Convention was ratified in 1990.

Bringing the Convention to life

UNICEF/95-0071/Shadid

Some of the most significant changes sparked by the Convention on the Rights of the Child are those now occurring in the legal systems of countries.

The measures range from broad endorsements of children's rights to the revision of laws and changes in national constitutions. Togo, for instance, has incorporated all operative articles of the Convention into its new Constitution. Other African countries that have introduced elements of the Convention into their Constitutions include Angola, Ethiopia, Namibia and Uganda. For example, Ethiopia's Constitution establishes the best interests of the child as a primary consideration.

South Africa's proposed Constitution recognizes, among others, the rights of children to a name, to basic nutrition, to education, to health and social services and to protection from exploitative labour practices. Eritrea's proposed Constitution also contains protections for children and families. Angola's Family Code sets out the equal responsibility of mothers and fathers for their children; the country's Family Tracing Law is the legal foundation for the efforts to reunite children and families separated by years of civil conflict.

In Honduras, the country's governing body unanimously approved a new detailed Children's Rights Code based on the Convention. The new Code, drafted over three years by members of non-governmental organizations (NGOs) and government ministries, came into force in September 1996, on Honduras' National Day for the Child. To implement the Code, training is being provided for 75 judges, 293 mayors and 300 staff of government institutions and NGOs.

In Uganda, the new Children's Statute, signed by President Yoweri Museveni in April 1996, is regarded by child rights advocates as a pioneering and historic step for Africa. Guided by the Convention, the Statute affirms the country's commitment to meeting the needs of its youngest citizens. Among other measures, it empowers local authorities to establish Family and Children Courts in every district, spells out foster care and adoption procedures, and establishes humane processes for the rehabilitation of juvenile offenders.

Tunisia's Code for the Protection of Children, adopted in October 1995, contains 123 articles that bring national laws into harmony with the Convention.

Nepal has also adopted comprehensive child rights legislation in its Children's Act. Child welfare boards, consisting of representatives of government ministries, NGOs and professional groups, are being created at both district and national levels to implement the Act.

Other countries that have passed legislation on child rights concerns include China, which enacted a law in 1995 that states that Chinese citizens, regardless of ethnic group, race, sex, age, occupation, property status or religious belief, have the right and obligation to receive education. St. Kitts and Nevis passed a law in 1994 establishing an agency to formulate policy and deliver services benefiting children. In Burkina Faso, a law has made child rights part of both primary and secondary curricula, and the country is establishing courts and appointing judges for children.

A schoolroom in Burkina Faso.

Labour, scheduled for October 1997 in Oslo, derive their impetus from the Convention. Highlighting the problems in this way is an essential first step towards their elimination.

In a positive initiative to involve the media in educating children about their rights, the Asian Summit on Child Rights and the Media, held in Manila in July 1996, included a wide range of participants in four days of discussions on how to educate, inform and entertain children while also taking into account their best interests.

UNICEF itself is at a turning-point. In its 50th year, the organization has adopted a mission statement that looks to the Convention as its guiding force.

This new mandate has important implications for the work of the organization. Its efforts for children in the past two decades, including the year 2000 goals established by the international community at the World Summit for Children in 1990, are designed to alleviate the worst aspects of poverty for the majority of the world's children. These goals and agreements must now be pursued in the context of the Convention.

In September 1996, the Secretary-General of the United Nations, Boutros Boutros-Ghali, reported to the General Assembly on the progress made in meeting the Summit's year 2000 goals for children as the decade for action passed the halfway mark. Much of the news is good, with millions of children's lives having been saved since 1990.

But much remains to be done. More than 12.5 million children under five in developing countries continue to die each year, 9 million of them from causes for which inexpensive solutions and measures such as immunization and antibiotics have been routinely applied in the industrialized world for 50 years.[2]

As long as preventable death and suffering continue on a large scale in the developing world, child survival must remain an urgent priority. But now, within the context of the Convention, UNICEF and the world community must not only maintain the commitment to the year 2000 goals but also look beyond them to social protection and other important needs and rights not expressly contained in the World Summit Declaration and Plan of Action. The Convention, by expressing and protecting all the rights of children, expands the scope of action required for children and throws a clear shaft of light on paths that extend beyond the year 2000.

Some of these will involve protecting children and youth in conflict with the criminal justice system; others will ensure the development of the young child, support families, end the use of land-mines and continue to try to bring about a more equitable distribution of resources.

It is in this context that *The State of the World's Children 1997* report explores the subject of child labour and its impact on children's development.

The Convention requires families, societies, governments and the international community to take action designed to fulfil the rights of all children in a sustainable, participatory and non-discriminatory manner. In practical terms, this means that the poorest, most vulnerable and often the most neglected children in all societies, rich and poor, must have first call on resources and efforts.

The endeavours to touch their lives will be complex and will require a sustained attack on the root causes of poverty and underdevelopment.

In a world where technology and knowledge are available and easy to share, and per capita income has tripled in the past quarter of a century,[3]

The world community must not only maintain the commitment to the year 2000 goals but also look beyond them to social protection and other important needs and rights.

Redirecting just one quarter of the developing world's military expenditure — or $30 billion of $125 billion — for example, could provide enough additional resources to reach most of the goals for the year 2000.

there can be no excuses: the rights of all children, including those who are most disadvantaged, can be fulfilled.

The international community has tried in this last decade of the 20th century to arrive at a consensus on the way forward on a number of fronts: on human rights, on protection of the environment, on reduction of uncontrolled population growth and on eliminating gender inequality. The avowed aim is sustainable development for all on the basis of social justice and human fulfilment.

Good intentions will now have to be matched with the political will to act and fortified by changes in individual and national attitudes and priorities. An additional $40 billion a year could ensure access for all the world's people to basic social services such as health care, education and safe water.[4]

Two thirds of this amount could be found by developing countries if they realigned their own budget priorities. Redirecting just one quarter of the developing world's military expenditure — or $30 billion of $125 billion[5] — for example, could provide enough additional resources to reach most of the goals for the year 2000. A similar shift in the targeting of development aid by donor countries could generate much of the rest.

This premise is set out in the 20/20 initiative, which calls for developing countries to increase government spending on basic social services from the current average of approximately 13 per cent to 20 per cent, and for donor countries to earmark 20 per cent of official development assistance (ODA).

This kind of shift in the way the world uses its resources is no longer an appeal to the charity of those with the power and the purse-strings but is a matter of rights and obligations. The new era in child rights will still need underpinning by attitudinal change, popular pressure and public demands.

Wherever opinion polls have been undertaken they have shown that people support the ideas and ideals of human rights, child rights and international solidarity. Part of the task, then, is to channel this support into action.

For the past 15 years, *The State of the World's Children* has mobilized public and political support for child survival and development. UNICEF will continue to mobilize, now with the added power and legitimacy of the Convention, because the need for passionate advocacy on behalf of the world's children has not diminished, even now, half a century after the need for UNICEF was internationally acknowledged.

As Philip Alston, a leading child rights lawyer and activist, states: "In the final analysis, appropriate policies will be adopted... only in response to widespread and insistent public outrage."

Chapter II

Children at risk:
Ending hazardous and exploitative child labour

In cottage industries throughout the world, all family members contribute. In Honduras, a young boy sleeps at the work table where he stitches softballs in his home.

Myth and reality

"Dust from the chemical powders and strong vapours in both the storeroom and the boiler room were obvious....We found 250 children, mostly below 10 years of age, working in a long hall filling in a slotted frame with sticks. Row upon row of children, some barely five years old, were involved in the work." [1]

The description could come from an observer appalled at the working conditions endured by children in the 19th century in British mills and factories.

The world, you feel, must surely have banished such obscenities to the distant past. But the quote is from a report on the matchstick-making industry of modern-day Sivakasi, in India.

And similar descriptions of children at work in hazardous conditions can be gathered from countries across the world. In Malaysia, children may work up to 17-hour days on rubber plantations, exposed to insect and snake bites. In the United Republic of Tanzania, they pick coffee, inhaling pesticides. In Portugal, children as young as 12 are subject to the heavy labour and myriad dangers of the construction industry. In Morocco, they hunch at looms for long hours and little pay, knotting the strands of luxury carpets for export. In the United States, children are exploited in garment industry sweatshops. In the Philippines, young boys dive in dangerous conditions to help set nets for deep-sea fishing.

The world should, indeed, have outgrown the many forms of abuse labouring children endure. But it hasn't, although not for lack of effort. Child labour was one of the first and most important issues addressed by the international community, resulting in the International Labour Organization's (ILO) 1919 Minimum Age Convention (Panel 3).

Early efforts were hobbled, in part, because campaigners struggling to end child labour appealed to morality and ethics, values easily sidelined by the drive for profit and the hard realities of commercial life. Child labourers were objects of charity or humanitarian concern but they had no legal rights.

Today's world is different at least in this respect. Children have rights established in international laws, not least in the Convention on the Rights

Among the most hazardous of jobs is scavenging. Children, like this boy in Brazil, collect used paper, plastics, rags and bottles from garbage dumps, selling them to retailers for recycling.

The world should, indeed, have outgrown the many forms of abuse labouring children endure. But it hasn't.

Fig. 1 Child labour: A look at the past

The industrialized world had significant numbers of children working, as recently as 100 years ago. The following charts show the composition of the workforce, in some cases approaching 50 per cent children. Working hours were often long. For instance, in Ghent industries in 1847, a child's work week was generally the same as an adult's: 13 hours per day, 78 hours per week. The charts do not reflect the unpaid work done by children at home.

Belgium, ca. 1850

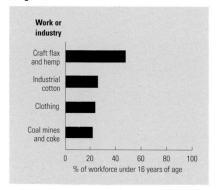

England and Wales, ca. 1850

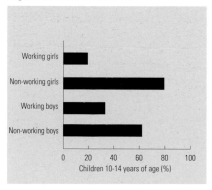

Japan, 1900

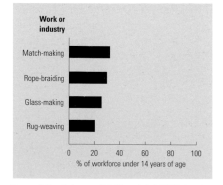

Source: H. Cunningham, and P.P. Viazzo (eds.), Child Labour in Historical Perspective, 1800-1985: Case studies from Europe, Japan and Colombia, UNICEF International Child Development Centre, Florence, 1996, pp. 27, 42, 78.

of the Child, which has now been ratified by all but a few countries. Ratification specifically obligates governments — in article 32 — to protect children "from economic exploitation and from performing any work that is likely to be hazardous or to interfere with the child's education, or to be harmful to the child's health or physical, mental, spiritual, moral or social development."

But beyond that article, children's exploitation in work contravenes many more of the rights enshrined in the Convention, among them children's rights to care by their parents, to compulsory and free primary education, to the highest attainable standard of health, to social security, and to provisions for rest and recreation. The rights of those children whose primary activity is work are, without question, in jeopardy.

Looking at children's work through the lens of children's rights and the Convention on the Rights of the Child, as this *State of the World's Children* report seeks to do, offers not only new ways of understanding the problem of child labour but also provides new impetus and direction to the movement against it.

As we will see, child labour is often a complex issue. Powerful forces sustain it, including many employers, vested interest groups and economists proposing that the market must be free at all costs, and traditionalists believing the caste or class of certain children denudes them of rights.

Our lodestar must always be the best interests of the child. It can never be in the best interests of a child to be exploited or to perform heavy and dangerous forms of work. No child should labour in hazardous and exploitative conditions, just as no child should die of preventable illnesses.

On this point there can be no doubt. Work that endangers children's physical, mental, spiritual, moral or social development must end. Hazardous child labour is a betrayal of every child's rights as a human being and is an offence against our civilization.

Four myths about child labour

The recent surge of interest in child labour has too often been founded upon — and contributed to — four myths about child labour that it is vital to confront. The first is that child labour is uniquely a problem of the developing world. The second is that child labour emerges inevitably and naturally out of poverty and thus will always be with us. The third is that most child labourers are at work in sweatshops producing cheap goods for export to the stores of the rich world. And the fourth is that there is a simple solution to the child labour problem — a 'trade sanction' or 'boycott' — that will end it once and for all.

Myth One

Child labour only happens in the poor world — While the vast majority of working children are found in developing countries, children routinely work in all countries. In every country, rich and poor, it is the **nature** of the work children do that determines whether or not they are harmed by it — not the plain fact of their working. Few people in the industrialized world, for example, would look upon the employment of a child to deliver newspapers for an hour or two before school as an exploitative form of child labour, despite the fact that the child will certainly be paid less than normal adult rates for the job. Often such a job will be encouraged in the interest of the child's gaining experience of the 'real world' of work and commerce.

Legislative landmarks

From the first international child labour convention (1919), which saw working children in terms of wage employment in formal-sector manufacturing, the world's position on child labour has evolved and expanded over the years. It has come to address non-industrial work by children, and most recently, to prohibit any kind of work, paid or unpaid, that is injurious to children, and to set out safeguards and protections for children who work. States parties to the Convention on the Rights of the Child, for example, are required to provide for a minimum age or minimum ages for admission to employment "having regard to the relevant provisions of other international instruments" (article 32). The laws outlined below are international landmarks in protecting children.

1919: Minimum Age (Industry) Convention No. 5. Adopted at the first session of the International Labour Organization (ILO) and ratified by 72 countries, the Convention established 14 years as the minimum age for children to be employed in industry. It was the first international effort to regulate children's participation in the workplace and was followed by numerous ILO instruments applicable to other economic sectors.

1930: ILO Forced Labour Convention No. 29 provides for the suppression of the use of forced or compulsory labour in all its forms. The term "forced or compulsory labour" is considered to mean all work or service exacted from any people under the threat of penalty and for which they have not offered themselves voluntarily. Ratifications: 139 States as of mid-September 1996.

1966: International Covenant on Civil and Political Rights. Adopted by the UN General Assembly in 1966 and entered into force in 1976, it reaffirms the principles of the Universal Declaration of Human Rights (1948) with regard to civil and political rights and commits States parties to take action to realize these rights. Article 8 states that no one should be kept in slavery or servitude or be required to perform forced or compulsory labour. Ratifications: 135 States as of mid-September 1996.

1966: International Covenant on Economic, Social and Cultural Rights. Adopted by the UN General Assembly in 1966 and entered into force in 1976, it reaffirms the principles of the Universal Declaration of Human Rights with regard to economic, social and cultural rights. Article 10 enjoins States parties to protect young people from economic exploitation and from employment in work harmful to their morals, their health or their lives, or likely to hamper their normal development. It also commits States parties to set age limits below which the paid employment of child labour should be prohibited and punishable by law. Ratifications: 135 States as of mid-September 1996.

1973: ILO Minimum Age Convention No. 138 supersedes prior instruments applicable to limited economic sectors. The Convention obliges member States to pursue a national policy designed to ensure the effective abolition of child labour. In this connection, it establishes that no child can be employed in any economic sector below the age designated for the completion of compulsory schooling — and not less than 15 years. The minimum age for admission to any work likely to jeopardize health, safety or morals is 18 years. Ratifications: 49 States as of mid-September 1996.

Minimum Age Recommendation No. 146 calls on States to raise the minimum age of employment to 16 years. While not legally obligating, it nonetheless is a strong call to action on the part of member States. Convention No. 138 and this Recommendation are regarded as the most comprehensive international instruments and statements on child labour.

1989: Convention on the Rights of the Child. Enshrines as interdependent and indivisible the full range of the civil, political, economic, social and cultural rights of all children that are vital to their survival, development, protection and participation in the lives of their societies. Because of this connection between children's rights and their survival and development, virtually all the Convention's articles address issues — such as education, health, nutrition, rest and relaxation, social security, the responsibilities of parents — that are related to child labour and its effects on children. One of the tenets of the Convention is that in all actions concerning children, their best interests should be taken fully into account. Article 32 recognizes children's right to be protected from work that threatens their health, education or development and enjoins States parties to set minimum ages for employment and to regulate working conditions. Ratifications: 187 States as of mid-September 1996.

1996: ILO proposes for discussion a new convention on hazardous child labour or the elimination of the most intolerable forms of child labour.

The long hours and strains of carpet-weaving cause muscular diseases and deformities, and the inhalation of carpet fibre and chemicals leads to respiratory infections. A boy in Afghanistan works at a loom.

UNICEF/5530/Isaac

This is also how children's work is regarded by many families in the developing world — with the difference that these families are often in dire need of the income or help their children can provide, whereas children in industrialized countries are often working for pocket money.

When all forms of work are considered, the percentage of children working in industrialized countries can be surprisingly high. In the United Kingdom, for example, the most reliable estimates available show that between 15 and 26 per cent of 11-year-olds and between 36 and 66 per cent of 15-year-olds are working.[2]

Most of these child workers in industrialized countries also attend school. But there is a naïvety in the assumption that the only kind of work undertaken by children in the West is on the 'pocket money' model. Industrialized nations tend to see themselves as having completely eradicated the harsher forms of child labour and thus preach that poorer countries should follow their example.

Yet hazardous forms of child labour can be found in most rich countries. Usually, the exploited children come from ethnic minorities or immigrant groups, as with the Gypsy and Albanian communities in Greece. In the US, for example, the majority of child workers are employed in agriculture, and a high proportion of them are from immigrant or ethnic-minority families. A study by the US General Accounting Office showed a 250 per cent increase in child labour violations between 1983 and 1990. In a three-day sting operation in 1990, the US Department of Labor discovered more than 11,000 children working illegally.[3] The same year, a survey of Mexican-American children working on New York state farms showed that almost half had worked in fields still wet with pesticides and more than a third had themselves been sprayed, either directly or indirectly.[4]

Myth Two

Child labour will never be eliminated until poverty disappears — It is true that the poorest, most disadvantaged sectors of society supply the vast majority of child labourers. The conclusion often drawn from this is that child labour and poverty are inseparable and that calls for an immediate end to hazardous child labour are unrealistic. We are told we must tolerate the intolerable until world poverty is ended.

This is very convenient for all those who benefit from the status quo. But it is also untrue. The fact remains that when a child is engaged in hazardous labour, someone — an employer, a customer or a parent — benefits from that labour. It is this element of exploitation that is overlooked by those who see child labour as inseparable from poverty. However poor their families may be, children would not be harmed by work if there were not people prepared and able to exploit them. And child labour, in fact, can actually perpetuate poverty, as a working child grows into an adult trapped in unskilled and badly paid jobs.

Of course, poverty must be reduced. Its reduction by economic growth, by employment generation and by investment, by better distribution of income, by changes in the global economy, as well as by better allocation of government budgets and better targeting of aid flows will reduce the potential pool of child labourers.

But hazardous child labour can and must be eliminated independently of wider measures aimed at poverty reduction.

At the highest level, governments have begun to move on the issue, to make good the commitments they assumed in ratifying the Convention on the Rights of the Child. In New Delhi in 1996, for example, labour ministers of the Non-Aligned Movement agreed that "exploitative child labour wherever it is practised is a moral outrage and an affront to human dignity." They resolved to give "immediate priority for total and de facto elimination of child labour in hazardous employments."[5] At the local level, activists' groups and non-governmental organizations (NGOs) are exploring ways to remove children from dangerous work situations and provide alternatives for them. And in August 1996, the third South Asian Association for Regional Cooperation (SAARC) Ministerial Conference on the Children of South Asia committed member States to ending bonded labour by the year 2000 and to "eliminate the evil of child labour" by 2010.

The end of hazardous child labour does not have to — and must not — wait for the end of poverty. World poverty cannot be eliminated by the end of the decade. But hazardous child labour — and the grave violation of the rights of the children involved — can be.

Myth Three

Child labour primarily occurs in export industries — Export industries are the most visible sector in which children work. Soccer balls made by children in Pakistan for use by children in industrialized countries may be a compelling symbol. But we must not lose sight of the tens of millions of children all around the world who work in non-export areas, often in hazardous or exploitative conditions. In fact, only a very small percentage of all child workers are employed in export-sector industries — probably less than 5 per cent.[6]

A 1995 study in Bangladesh, for example, revealed that children were active in more than 300 different kinds of jobs outside the export sector. These ranged from household work to brick-making, from stone-breaking to selling in shops and on streets, from bike-repairing to garbage-collecting and rag-picking.[7] What is more, this assessment took into account only jobs done in cities. Most children work on farms and plantations or houses, far from the reach of labour inspectors and from media scrutiny.

If we allow the notion that the most exploited child workers are **all** in the industrial export sector to take hold, we would do a grave disservice to that great majority of children who labour in virtual invisibility.

Myth Four

The only way to make headway against child labour is for consumers and governments to apply pressure through sanctions and boycotts — This is incorrect on two counts. First, it implies that all the momentum for action on child labour is generated by Western pressure — and that people, NGOs, the media and governments in developing countries have been ignoring or condoning the problem. In fact, activists and organizations, both local and international, have been diligently at work in developing countries for years, exposing child labour abuses, developing local and national programmes and promoting consumer awareness in their own countries and in the West through international campaigns.

The ILO International Programme on the Elimination of Child Labour is one important example. Launched in 1991 to help children in six countries, it now works with NGO and government partners in 19 countries (Panel 4). To cite just two others, in a UNICEF-assisted programme in the Philippines, teams composed of gov-

The end of hazardous child labour does not have to — and must not — wait for the end of poverty.

IPEC partnerships for children

UNICEF/Halevi

I n Brazil, trade unions have publicized the problems of child labour and have managed to secure child labour clauses in contracts with employers in 88 municipalities in 8 federal states. In northern Thailand, the Daughters' Education Programme is helping young girls in 70 communities with basic non-formal education, counselling and skills training and alerting them, their families, their teachers and the leaders of their communities to the dangers that prostitution poses.

These are only two examples of how the International Labour Organization's (ILO) International Programme on the Elimination of Child Labour (IPEC) is working to end hazardous and exploitative child labour. IPEC has distinguished itself with its creative and flexible approach, tailored to fit children's needs and countries' capacities. It has also earned respect for reinforcing the national commitment and structures on which permanent improvements depend.

Launched in 1991 with a grant from the German Government, IPEC currently has 19 participating countries — Bangladesh, Bolivia, Brazil, Chile, Costa Rica, Egypt, El Salvador, Guatemala, India, Indonesia, Kenya, Nepal, Nicaragua, Pakistan, Panama, the Philippines, Tanzania, Thailand and Turkey. Another 10 countries are preparing to launch the programme.

An IPEC programme begins with the signing of a Memorandum of Understanding between the government and ILO, detailing areas of cooperation. Studies and surveys define the nature and magnitude of child labour problems in a country, and together with consultations, form the base on which the national plan of action is created.

Once a country's plan is developed, government agencies, employers' and workers' organizations, NGOs, universities and the media carry it out. Since no single organization or strategy can offer a complete solution to the problem of child labour, partnerships and alliances are vital. A country establishes a committee to coordinate the various participating groups and oversee the programme's management. This involvement of many partners both strengthens a nation's capacity to effect change and builds a sense of country ownership of IPEC programmes.

Another essential element of the IPEC approach is to create awareness of the dangers and extent of child labour. The message is spread in various ways, such as radio programming, which has proven to be a powerful and cost-effective tool, particularly in rural areas. In Thailand, cartoon and picture books describe the dangers of child labour.

IPEC also helps countries strengthen legislation and enforcement and monitoring capacities. Many countries have started training labour inspectors as they are often the only ones who can gain access to 'invisible' child workers. A field-tested labour inspection manual developed by IPEC is now available in several languages. Programmes also focus on other broader legislative issues, such as reconciling labour and education laws to ensure that the minimum age for employment in a country is higher than the age at which a child completes compulsory education.

Education and awareness-raising are often complementary components of programmes. In India, for example, when the Centre for Rural Education and Development Association (CREDA), supported by the Indian Government and IPEC, conducted a wide awareness campaign among community members, loom owners and children, more than 4,500 child workers left the carpet industry. The 68 centres for non-formal learning that CREDA has set up in the area give the children a basic grounding in life skills and vocational training, nutrition, health and child rights. As a result of strong parental and community support, many other children were released from looms; an additional 1,500 at-risk children were admitted to government schools.

The needs of children who combine work with school are also addressed by IPEC. In Indonesia, for example, learning materials have been developed for use in a large government-funded non-formal education programme. The curriculum includes subjects such as literacy, numeracy, basic housekeeping, hygiene and life skills set out in a teacher's guide and trainee booklets. Several ILO-IPEC implementing agencies have started to use the materials.

None of these innovations would be possible without the support of IPEC's donors, which include Australia, Belgium, Canada, France, Germany, Luxembourg, Norway and the United States. Last year, the Government of Spain provided a grant to expand IPEC to 13 countries in Latin America.

The IPEC budget is small, and programme costs seem especially low when weighed against the benefits: better lives and futures for children.

Photo: Vocational training is a part of many IPEC programmes. In Thailand, a boy sews garments.

ernment inspectors, social workers, police, NGOs, prosecutors and the media regularly investigate working children's conditions, removing those in danger. And in Bangladesh, where primary education is a high priority, a joint NGO/government non-formal education programme for 1.4 million poor urban children was designed in late 1995.

Second, this myth implies that there is one clear highway, usually involving trade sanctions and consumer boycotts, speeding a newly impassioned global society all the way to the resolution of the problem.

International commitment and pressure are undoubtedly important. But sanctions affect only export industries, which, as we have seen, exploit a relatively small percentage of child labourers. And sanctions are also blunt instruments with long-term consequences that may not be foreseen, with the result that they harm, instead of help, children.

The Harkin Bill, which was introduced into the US Congress in 1992 with the laudable aim of prohibiting the import of products made by children under 15, is a case in point. As of September 1996, the Bill had yet to find its way onto the statute books. But the mere threat of such a measure panicked the garment industry of Bangladesh, 60 per cent of whose products — some $900 million in value — were exported to the US in 1994.[8]

Child workers, most of them girls, were summarily dismissed from the garment factories. A study sponsored by international organizations took the unusual step of tracing some of these children to see what happened to them after their dismissal. Some were found working in more hazardous situations, in unsafe workshops where they were paid less, or in prostitution.

Iolanda Huzak

A boy feeds a charcoal furnace in Mato Grosso do Sul (Brazil).

**Fig. 2 The world's children:
How many, how old?**

The world's children (0-18 years) number over 2
billion. Nearly 9 out of 10 of them (87 per cent) live
in developing countries.

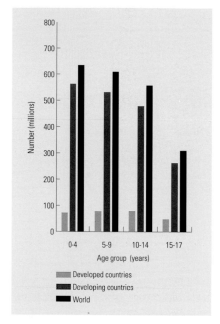

Source: UN Population Division, World Population Prospects:
The 1994 revision, United Nations, New York, 1995.

This, then, was a classic case of
good motives gone wrong. However,
not all was lost. A ground-breaking
agreement was reached to protect the
affected children (Panel 12).

A clear lesson can be learned in all
of this. Because of their potential to
do harm, in any situation where sanctions are contemplated, a child-impact
assessment would need to be made at
the point of application, and constant
monitoring would be needed thereafter to gauge the long-term effects on
children.

What is child labour?

It is time to define terms. The phrase
'child labour' conjures up a particular
image: we see children chained to
looms in dark mills and sweatshops,
as if in a long and nightmarish line
running from Lancashire in the 1830s
right through to the South Asia of the
1990s.

In reality, children do a variety of
work in widely divergent conditions.
This work takes place along a continuum. At one end of the continuum, the
work is beneficial, promoting or enhancing a child's physical, mental,
spiritual, moral or social development
without interfering with schooling,
recreation and rest.

At the other end, it is palpably destructive or exploitative. There are
vast areas of activity between these
two poles, including work that need
not impact negatively on the child's
development.

At the most destructive end, no one
would publicly argue that exploiting
children as prostitutes is acceptable in
any circumstances. The same can be
said about 'bonded child labour', the
term widely used for the virtual en-
slavement of children to repay debts
incurred by their parents or grandpar-
ents. This also applies to industries
notorious for the dire health and

safety hazards they present: for example, the charcoal furnaces in the
Brazilian state of Mato Grosso do Sul,
or the glass-bangle factories of
Firozabad in India. Hazardous work is
simply intolerable for all children.

But to treat all work by children as
equally unacceptable is to confuse
and trivialize the issue and to make it
more difficult to end the abuses. This
is why it is important to distinguish
between beneficial and intolerable
work and to recognize that much child
labour falls into a grey area between
these two extremes.

A decade ago, UNICEF deter-
mined that child labour is exploitative
if it involves:

► full-time work at too early an age;

► too many hours spent working;

► work that exerts undue physical,
social or psychological stress;

► work and life on the streets in bad
conditions;

► inadequate pay;

► too much responsibility;

► work that hampers access to
education;

► work that undermines children's
dignity and self-esteem, such as slavery or bonded labour and sexual
exploitation;

► work that is detrimental to full social and psychological development.[9]

The impact of work on a child's
development is the key to determining
when such work becomes a problem.
Work that is harmless to adults can
be extremely harmful to children.
Among the aspects of a child's development that can be endangered by
work are:

► physical development — including
overall health, coordination, strength,
vision and hearing;

► cognitive development — including literacy, numeracy and the acqui-
sition of knowledge necessary to
normal life;

► emotional development — including adequate self-esteem, family attachment, feelings of love and acceptance;

► social and moral development — including a sense of group identity, the ability to cooperate with others and the capacity to distinguish right from wrong.[10]

The physical harm is, of course, the easiest to see. Carrying heavy loads or sitting for long periods in unnatural positions can permanently disable growing bodies. Hard physical labour over a period of years can stunt children's physical stature by up to 30 per cent of their biological potential, as they expend stores of stamina that should last into adulthood.[11]

Children are also vulnerable psychologically: they can suffer devastating psychological damage from being in an environment in which they are demeaned or oppressed. Self-esteem is as important for children as it is for adults.

Education is one of the keys that will unlock the prison cell of hazardous labour in which so many children are confined. It is almost impossible to overemphasize this point.

Education helps a child develop cognitively, emotionally and socially, and it is an area often gravely jeopardized by child labour. Work can interfere with education in the following ways:

► it frequently absorbs so much time that school attendance is impossible;

► it often leaves children so exhausted that they lack the energy to attend school or cannot study effectively when in class;

► some occupations, especially seasonal agricultural work, cause children to miss too many days of class even though they are enrolled in school;

► the social environment of work sometimes undermines the value children place on education, something to

which street children are particularly vulnerable;

► children mistreated in the workplace may be so traumatized that they cannot concentrate on school work or are rejected by teachers as disruptive.[12]

How old is a child?

All cultures share the view that the younger the children, the more vulnerable they are physically and psychologically and the less they are able to fend for themselves. Age limits are a formal reflection of society's judgement about the evolution of children's capacities and responsibilities.

Almost everywhere, age limits formally regulate children's activities: when they can leave school; when they can marry; when they can vote; when they can be treated as adults by the criminal-justice system; when they can join the armed forces — and when they can work.

But age limits differ from activity to activity and from country to country. The legal minimum age for all work in Egypt, for example, is 12, in the Philippines 14, in Hong Kong 15. Peru adopts a variety of standards: the minimum age is 14 in agriculture; 15 in industry; 16 in deep-sea fishing; and 18 for work in ports and seafaring.[13]

Many countries make a distinction between light and hazardous work, with the minimum age for the former generally being 12, for the latter usually varying between 16 and 18.[14] The ILO Minimum Age Convention also broadly adopts this approach, allowing light work at age 12 or 13, but hazardous work not before 18.[15]

Nevertheless, ILO also establishes a general minimum age of 15 years — provided 15 is not less than the age of completion of compulsory schooling. This is the most widely used yardstick

Fig. 3 The working child: 1 out of every 4 in the developing world

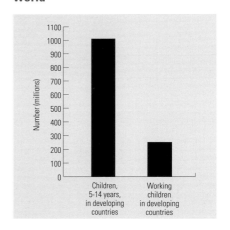

Fig. 4 Long days, long weeks

Of the projected 190 million working children in the 10-14 age group in the developing world, three quarters of them work six days a week or more and one half work nine hours a day or more.

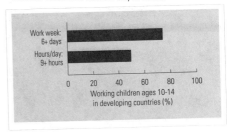

Note: Because of the scarcity of data on child labour, Figs. 3 and 4 represent projections of the numbers of the developing world's working children and of their hours, based on ILO surveys in specific countries.

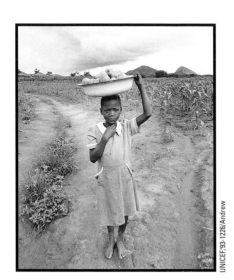

HIV/AIDS has resulted in greater numbers of children as heads of household who must fend for themselves. A girl in Malawi, one of nine children in a family orphaned by AIDS, carries a bowl full of mangoes.

when establishing how many children are currently working around the world.

How many children work?

Nobody knows for sure. ILO, one authority on the subject, considers the existing statistics vastly inadequate and unreliable and the process of data collection fraught with complications. A recent ILO limited survey, which indicated that 73 million of the world's children are employed — equivalent to 13 per cent of those aged 10 to 14[16] — helps illustrate some of the problems.

The survey was limited for many reasons. Many national governments did not respond. It did not include children at work in industrialized nations. It did not count the millions of child workers believed to be under 10 years of age, nor those employed in the informal sector, or attending school who might also be working. Nor did it include the biggest group of invisible workers: all those children — mainly girls — who are engaged in domestic labour, whether for their own families or as servants.

The collection of solid and reliable data regarding child labour is limited also by the fact that, in certain instances, it is presumed officially not to exist and therefore is not included in surveys or covered by official statistics. Further uncounted child labourers can be discovered if we surmise that children currently not enrolled in or attending school are working in some form or another. In India alone that would add some 90 million children, most of them girls, to the total. So, while it is impossible to cite a single authoritative figure, it is clear that the number of child workers worldwide runs into hundreds of millions (Fig. 3).

ILO, to better quantify the problem, recently launched experimental surveys in Ghana, India, Indonesia and Senegal, which employed local statisticians to study a sample of about 4,000 households and 200 businesses in each country. The results showed that the average percentage of economically active children aged between 5 and 14 was 25 per cent, and in Senegal it was as high as 40 per cent.[17]

Worldwide, the big picture looks something like this: the vast majority of all child labourers live in Asia, Africa and Latin America. Half of them can be found in Asia alone, although their proportion may be declining in South-East Asia as per capita income increases, basic education spreads and family size decreases. Africa has an average of one in three children working.[18] In Latin America, one child in five works.[19] These proportions have increased partly due to the economic crisis of the 1980s and, in Africa, because of the lack of public investment in education as well as because of armed conflict. In both Africa and Latin America, only a tiny proportion of child workers are involved in the formal sector. The vast majority work for their families, in homes, in the fields and on the streets.

Child labour has increased substantially in Central and Eastern European countries as a result of the abrupt switch from centrally planned to market economies. In industrialized countries, such as the UK and the US, meanwhile, the growth of the service sector and the quest for a more flexible workforce have contributed to an expansion of child labour. Political unrest and HIV/AIDS in African countries have resulted in increased reliance on child labour.

To see behind this big picture, the need for reliable measurements of the prevalence of child labour, according to internationally agreed definitions, is paramount. Governments, NGOs and international institutions need to work together on this massive task.

Above all, we need to know how many children are involved in detrimental work, at the worst end of the continuum. This is the group of children that policies and programmes need to reach most urgently.

Without this clearer information, the true scale of the problem will remain unknown. What has long hidden in the shadows will only emerge into the light, fully and finally, when we can measure it, and thus systematically move to eradicate it.

The roots of child labour

Most children who work do not have the power of free choice. They are not choosing between career options with varying advantages, drawbacks and levels of pay. A fortunate minority have sufficient material means behind them to be pulled towards work as an attractive option offering them even more economic advantages. But the vast majority are pushed into work that is often damaging to their development by three key factors: the exploitation of poverty; the absence of education; and the restrictions of tradition.

The exploitation of poverty

The most powerful force driving children into hazardous, debilitating labour is the exploitation of poverty. Where society is characterized by poverty and inequity, the incidence of child labour is likely to increase, as does the risk that it is exploitative.

For poor families, the small contribution of a child's income or assistance at home that allows the parents to work can make the difference between hunger and a bare sufficiency. Survey after survey makes this clear. A high proportion of child employees give their entire wages to their parents. Children's work is considered essential to maintaining the economic level of the household (Figs. 5 and 6). A review of nine Latin American countries has shown that without the income of working children aged 13-17, the incidence of poverty would rise by between 10 and 20 per cent.[20]

If employers were not prepared to exploit children there would be no child labour. The parents of child labourers are often unemployed or underemployed, desperate for secure employment and income. Yet it is not they but their children who are offered the jobs. Why? Because children can be paid less, of course. (In Latin America, for example, children aged 13-17 earn on average half the pay of a wage-earning adult with 7 years of education.[21]) Because children are more malleable: they will do what they are told without questioning authority. Because children are more powerless: they are less likely to organize against oppression and can be physically abused without striking back.

Put simply, children are employed because they are easier to exploit. Many employers, if challenged, will plead their own relative poverty and their need to pay the lowest wages in order to compete and survive. Others are more unashamed about their role, seeing the exploitation of children's work as a natural and necessary part of the existing social order. Owners of bonded labourers quoted by an Indian researcher, for example, believed that low-caste children should work rather than go to school. "Once they are allowed to come up to an equal level, nobody will go to the fields. Fields will be left uncultivated everywhere. We have to keep them under our

Fig. 5 Family purchasing power falls in many regions

Children can be forced into hazardous labour when family income and purchasing power decrease and parents cannot provide for their needs. The drop in purchasing power since 1990 has been dramatic in the Russian Federation and in some neighbouring countries in Asia. Families are growing poorer in sub-Saharan Africa and have lost economic ground recently in the Middle East and North Africa also.

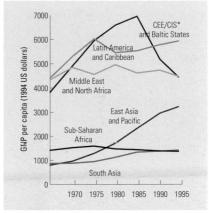

* Central and Eastern Europe/Commonwealth of Independent States

Fig. 6 Purchasing power: Industrialized vs. developing countries

The gap continues to widen between strong industrialized economies and those in the developing world.

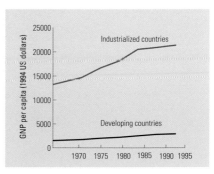

Note: These charts reflect local purchasing power in constant 1994 prices based on per capita gross national product (GNP). South Africa's GNP is not included in the sub-Saharan data.

Source for both figures: World Bank 1995 data.

In half of 14 countries surveyed, classrooms for grade 1 have sitting places for only 4 in 10 pupils. Half the pupils have no textbooks. Half the classrooms have no chalkboards.

strong thumb in order to get work done."[22]

Exploitation of the poor and the powerless not only means that adults are denied jobs that could better have sustained their families. It not only means that children are required to work in arduous, dangerous conditions. It also means a life of unskilled work and ignorance not only for the child but often for the children of generations to come. Any small, short-term financial gain for the family is at the cost of an incalculable long-term loss. Poverty begets child labour begets lack of education begets poverty.

Yet, poverty is not an eternal verity. It is sustained or diminished by political and economic policies and opportunities. Unfortunately, both national and international economic developments in recent decades have served to increase inequality and poverty.

The 1980s marked a serious downturn in the fortunes of many developing countries, as government indebtedness, unwise internal economic policies and recession resulted in economic crisis. The World Bank and the International Monetary Fund (IMF) responded by imposing on indebted nations, in return for loan guarantees, a package of policy prescriptions known as structural adjustment programmes. These sweeping economic reforms aimed to orient countries towards the needs of the global economy, promoting export crops and offering incentives to foreign investors while at the same time slashing government expenditure. All too often, the cuts in expenditure fell on health and education, on food subsidies and on social services, all needed most by the poor.

Firsthand experience in most countries shows that the real cost of adjustment is being paid disproportionately by the poor and by their children. It is also being paid by increasing numbers of child labourers. In Zimbabwe, for example, both government and ILO reports have linked the explosion of child labour directly to the impact of the country's structural adjustment programme.[23]

Gradually, structural adjustment programmes have been modified in an attempt to mitigate their effects on the vulnerable. In new agreements being concluded between governments and the international financial institutions, public expenditure on primary education and other basic social services is increasingly being protected from budget cuts. But most developing countries are still living with the policies of the recent past: unmodified adjustment packages still impact heavily on their poorest citizens. And it is in this state that they must now face the implications of the worldwide scramble for competitiveness associated with 'globalization'.

And many still concentrate scarce resources on military rather than social priorities. Sub-Saharan Africa now spends around $8 billion annually on the military, despite the fact that 216 million people in the region live in poverty. Similarly, South Asia — with 562 million in poverty — spent $14 billion on the military in 1994.[24]

A serious attack on poverty will reduce the number of children vulnerable to exploitation at work. Social safety nets are essential for the poor, as are access to credit and income-generating schemes, technology, education and basic health services. Budgetary priorities need to be re-examined and redirected in this light.

Tackling the exploitation itself does not have to wait until some future day when world poverty has been brought to an end. Hazardous child labour provides the most powerful of arguments for equality and social justice. It can and must be abolished here and now.

The lack of relevant education

Cuts in social spending have hit education — the most important single step in ending child labour — particularly hard.

In all regions, spending per student for higher education fell during the 1980s, and in Africa and Latin America, spending per pupil also fell for primary education.

A pilot survey, sponsored by the United Nations Educational, Scientific and Cultural Organization (UNESCO) and UNICEF and carried out in 1994 in 14 of the world's least developed countries, reinforced concerns about the actual conditions of primary schools. In half of these countries, classrooms for grade 1 have sitting places for only 4 in 10 pupils. Half the pupils have no textbooks and half the classrooms have no chalkboards. Teachers commonly have to attempt to handle huge classes — an average of 67 pupils per teacher in Bangladesh and nearly 90 per teacher in Equatorial Guinea. In 10 of the 14 countries, most children are taught in a language not spoken at home. And most homes, of course, have no books or magazines in any language.[25]

Education is clearly underfunded, but the school system as it stands in most developing countries is blighted by more than just a lack of resources. It is too often rigid and uninspiring in approach, promoting a curriculum that is irrelevant to and remote from children's lives.

The quality of teaching is frequently abysmal and the discipline violent, as 11-year-old Sudhir from Kone in India can testify: "In school, teachers would not teach well. If we ask them to teach us alphabets, they would beat us. They would sleep in the class. If we asked them about a small doubt, they would beat us and send us out. Even if we did not understand, they would not teach us. So I dropped out of school."

Sudhir's decision to drop out of school is hardly surprising. And that decision — often made by parents — is mirrored worldwide. Overall, 30 per cent of children in developing countries who enrol in primary school do not complete it.[26] The figure rises to 60 per cent in some countries. In Latin America, enrolment in school is comparatively high, yet only half those who enter school finish it, broadly the same proportion as in Africa with its much lower levels of enrolment. Even Brazil, one of the richest countries in the region, has a primary school completion rate of only 40 per cent.[27]

Education has become part of the problem. It has to be reborn as part of the solution.

Traditional expectations

The economic forces that propel children into hazardous work may be the most powerful of all. But traditions and entrenched social patterns play a part, too.

In industrialized countries, it is now almost universally accepted that if children are to develop normally and healthily, then they must not perform disabling work. In theory at least, education, play and leisure, friends, good health and proper rest must all have an important place in their lives.

This idea emerged only relatively recently. In the early decades of industrialization, work was thought to be the most effective way of teaching children about life and the world. Some residue of this notion remains in the widespread expectation that teenage children should take on casual jobs alongside school, both to gain an understanding of the way the world functions and to earn spending money of their own.

A girl in Niger goes about her chores.

UNICEF/93-1956/Pirozzi

29

Child domestic work:
Hidden exploitation

UNICEF/95-0647/Toutounji

Worldwide, millions of children toil in obscurity in private homes, behind closed doors, as domestic workers. One of the most widespread and least researched forms of child exploitation, domestic work holds many risks for the children — 9 out of 10 of them are girls — who are trapped in a cycle of dreary tasks amounting often to virtual slavery.

Because such work is largely hidden, its true extent is difficult to gauge, but recent studies have helped define the problem more clearly. In Jakarta (Indonesia), a survey discovered that almost one third of all domestic workers — about 400,000 — are under 15. Haiti has an estimated 250,000 child domestics, 20 per cent of whom are 7 to 10 years old.

Children work as domestics in Africa, Asia, Latin America, the Middle East and parts of southern Europe. Several factors are believed to have precipitated increasing numbers of children into this form of labour over

the past decade or so. The entry of more women into formal and informal labour markets, together with cutbacks in social services in many countries, has created a larger demand for domestic workers, and women and more and more children from impoverished families, including those families driven by poverty from rural to urban areas seeking employment, are a ready source of such workers. Once seen by many as an arrangement of 'patronage', child domestic work should be acknowledged for what it has become: the exploitation of child labour.

Children are employed by wealthy families and by families of modest income also, but living and work conditions are inappropriate in either case. The children are often expected to sleep where they can, on the kitchen floor or in the corner of a child's room. They may live for days on bread and tea and they endure scoldings and beatings. In Togo, for instance, an overwhelming majority of children

surveyed left previous domestic jobs because of a "cruel boss." Child domestics are exposed to emotional and sexual abuse by household members, deprived of their parents' affection and support, and exposed to humiliation by the children of their employers, all of which can deeply affect their self-esteem.

The hours are long. Child domestics in Jakarta work 12 to 15 hours a day. In Dhaka (Bangladesh), half the children interviewed in one study work even longer — 15 to 18 hours. Along with regular chores, like laundry, cooking, cleaning, and minding their employers' children, they are often on call into the night, bringing refreshments and polishing shoes, at the whim of all household members.

They earn little, and girls consistently earn less than boys. Sometimes the only remuneration is leftover food and discarded clothing. A recent survey in Kenya showed that 78 per cent of child domestics report payment "in kind," usually in the form of the occasional new dress or shoes. Only 17 per cent say they are paid in cash.

Few ever attend school. In Benin, for example, only 10 per cent received any formal education, leaving them trapped without skills or options. By drawing on and thus helping sustain a reservoir of uneducated young girls, domestic service in turn perpetuates the problems of poverty and lack of opportunity so deeply associated with the gender gap. In Dhaka, for example, only about 10 per cent of girl domestics are interested in education.

In the Dominican Republic, a child domestic is known as a '*puerta cerrada*', or 'closed door' servant. In Bangladesh, they are the 'tied down'. Their isolation can be almost complete, enduring as they do separation from parents, often for months at a time. In Dhaka, over half of those surveyed see their parents once every nine months or even less often. According to a worker at the Maurice Sixto Shelter for child domestic workers in Port-au-Prince (Haiti), 80 per cent of the children she sees suffer illnesses — upset stomachs, headaches — from emotional trauma.

Few programmes address the multiple developmental risks that child domestic workers face. The Maurice Sixto Shelter is one such programme, aiding 300 child domestics working in a Port-au-Prince suburb. Shelter workers gain the employers' consent to unite child domestics as often as possible with their natural families. The child workers attend nonformal classes with other children in the afternoon.

Another programme is the Sinaga Women and Child Labour Resource Centre in Nairobi (Kenya). Opened in 1994, it hopes to better the lives of some of Kenya's estimated 200,000 child domestic workers by providing basic education classes and skills training (Panel 6).

Domestic work represents grave risks and potential damage to children's development. The world is obliged to recognize and acknowledge these risks and ensure that these invisible workers are allowed to enjoy their childhood and their rights.

Photo: Two girls in the courtyard of the Maurice Sixto Shelter in Haiti, where young domestic workers receive basic education and psychological counselling.

There is a darker side to the expectations about children's work. The harder and more hazardous the jobs become, the more they are likely to be considered traditionally the province of the poor and disadvantaged, the lower classes and ethnic minorities. In India, for example, the view has been that some people are born to rule and to work with their minds while others, the vast majority, are born to work with their bodies. Many traditionalists have been unperturbed about lower-caste children failing to enrol in or dropping out of school. And if those children end up doing hazardous labour, it is likely to be seen as their lot in life.[28]

The rigidity of the caste system in India only dramatizes what is true in most of the world, including the West. The dominant cultural group may not wish its own children to do hazardous labour, but it will not be so concerned if young people from racial, ethnic or economic minorities do it. In northern Europe, for example, child labourers are likely to be African or Turkish. In the US, they are Asian or Latin American; in Canada, they are Asian. In Brazil, they tend to be the descendants of slaves or the children of indigenous people with no political clout. In Argentina, many are Bolivian and Paraguayan. In Thailand's fishing industry, many are from Myanmar.

And as traditional forces push children into work in many parts of the world, the situation is worsened by the growing culture of consumerism.

Understanding all the various cultural factors that lead children into work is essential. But deference to tradition is often cited as a reason for not acting against intolerable forms of child labour. Children have an absolute, unnegotiable right to freedom from hazardous child labour — a right now established in international law and accepted by every country that

The harder and more hazardous the jobs become, the more they are likely to be considered traditionally the province of the poor and disadvantaged, the lower classes and ethnic minorities.

Child domestic workers are very often cut off from the community, denied rest and play. In Lima (Peru), a survey estimated that nearly a third of domestic workers never leave the home where they work.

has ratified the Convention on the Rights of the Child. Respect for diverse cultures should not deflect us from using all the means at our disposal to make every society, every economy, every corporation, regard the exploitation of children as unthinkable.

The shapes of child labour

The many manifestations of child labour can be broken down into seven main types, none of which are unique to any one region of the world. These are domestic service, forced and bonded labour, commercial sexual exploitation, industrial and plantation work, street work, work for the family and girls' work.

Domestic service

Child domestic workers are the world's most forgotten children, which is why it is worth considering their plight before that of other, more familiar groups of child workers (Panel 5). Although domestic service need not be hazardous, most of the time it is just that. Children in domestic servitude may well be the most vulnerable and exploited children of all, as well as the most difficult to protect. They are often extremely poorly paid or not paid at all; their terms and conditions are very often entirely at the whim of the employers and take no account of their legal rights; they are deprived of schooling, play and social activity, and of emotional support from family and friends. They are vulnerable to physical and sexual abuse. What more miserable situation could there be for a child — sometimes as young as age five — than to experience such conditions among often hostile strangers?

Consider, for example, a day in the life of seven-year-old Marie, from

Haiti. She is a *restavek* — Creole for *rester avec* — the local term for a type of child domestic found all over the world, one who has been handed over by a poor rural family to live with and provide domestic 'help' for a usually urban, wealthier family. She gets up at five in the morning and begins her day by fetching water from a nearby well, balancing the heavy jug on her head as she returns. She prepares breakfast and serves it to the members of the household. Then she walks the family's five-year-old son to school; later, at noon, she brings him home and helps him change clothes.

Next, she helps prepare and serve the family's lunch before returning the boy to school. In between meal times she must buy food in the market and run errands, tend the charcoal fire, sweep the yard, wash clothes and dishes, clean the kitchen and — at least once a day — wash her female boss's feet. She is given leftovers or cornmeal to eat, has ragged clothes and no shoes and sleeps outdoors or on the floor. She is not allowed to bathe in the water she brings to the household. She is regularly beaten with a leather strap if she is slow to respond to a request or is considered disrespectful. Needless to say, she is not allowed to attend school.[29]

The very nature of domestic work means that those doing it are shut away from the eyes of the world, unprotected from abuse. As we have seen, this isolation also makes it difficult to establish reliable estimates of the number of children involved. Some idea of the scale of the problem can, however, be gleaned from local surveys.

A survey of middle-income households in Colombo (Sri Lanka) showed that one in three had a child under 14 years of age as a domestic worker. A study of a lower-middle-class residential area in Nairobi (Kenya) found that

20 per cent of households employed children in 1982, though by 1991 this had dropped to 12 per cent, perhaps due to falling living standards. A survey of domestic workers in Uruguay found that 34 per cent had begun working before they were 14.[30] A survey in India, noting that 17 per cent of domestic workers were under 15 years old, reported that girls aged 12 to 15 were the preferred choice of 90 per cent of employing households.[31] Children are often preferred to adults precisely because they can be dominated more easily and, of course, paid less.

The impact of a life like Marie's on a child's development is profound. An obvious negative is poor nutrition, since it is rare that child domestics share equally in the family meals. A Peruvian girl says: "They would give us two rolls to eat with tea. After that I used to go to bed. Meanwhile they were eating buttered toast, coffee with milk, steak, and on top of that, grapes, pears, apples and peaches."[32] The evidence is not just anecdotal: a study of 15-year-old *restaveks* in Haiti compared them with other local children and found them on average 4 centimetres shorter and 18 kilograms lighter.[33]

Sexual abuse is often regarded by the employer as part of the employment terms. Jeanne, a 15-year-old working in Cotonou (Benin), has the normal heavy workload, is unpaid and is beaten when her employers are dissatisfied with her work. But her greatest problem is the family's 23-year-old son, who rapes her regularly. If she resists, he creates situations that lead to her being beaten.[34]

Even when not sexually abused, child domestics can suffer severe damage in terms of their psychological and social development. They are very often cut off from the community, denied rest and play. In Lima (Peru), a survey estimated that nearly a third of domestic workers never leave the home where they work.[35] Haitian psychologists who have worked with *restaveks* describe conditions of depression, passivity, sleep and eating disorders, as well as chronic fear and anxiety.[36] Among the most common adjectives used to describe child domestic workers are 'timid' and 'listless'. Childhood has been stolen from these children.

Research in this field is still in its infancy. But to promote it, early in 1996 Anti-Slavery International organized a seminar at Charney Manor, Oxfordshire (UK) for NGOs and institutes that have investigated the situation of children in domestic service. Supported financially by ILO-IPEC and by UNICEF, participants came from Bangladesh and Nepal in South Asia, Indonesia and the Philippines in South-East Asia, Kenya in East Africa, Senegal and Togo in West Africa, Haiti in the Caribbean and Guatemala in Central America — eloquent testimony to the extent of the problem. Several major common themes emerged:

► "There is no problem." In virtually all countries where children carry the burdens of household work, society does not regard it as a reprehensible practice. Even some of the activists at the seminar were not convinced that the practice itself — as opposed to its most exploitative forms — was damaging.

► Access to children working in homes is very difficult. Several researchers reported obstruction from employers. Even where access was obtained, it was difficult to conduct meaningful interviews with children when employers insisted on remaining present.

► The need for accurate estimates of the numbers of child domestics and the conditions under which they work was emphasized. Information about

Family work, the most common of all labour done by children, may be beneficial and give children a sense of self-worth. But it may demand too much of children, even keeping them from school. A girl, 12 years old, in Bangladesh, helps with the household chores.

Kenyan girls find hope at Sinaga

UNICEF/ESARO/Pirozzi

Christine, age 11, cheeks flushed with heat, gingerly lifts a hot tray from the oven and displays her baking — a dozen glistening buns, Christine's first success in her first cooking lesson. They are also an important part of Christine's job training.

Christine is one of the thousands of domestic child workers who provide the labour in the urban households of Kenya, allowing the wife or female head of the household to work for income outside the home.

Very often these girl workers are related to the employer, children of brothers, sisters and cousins in the rural areas. The rural family is only too glad to be relieved of the responsibility of feeding a child. And usually, the relative undertakes to educate the child.

Once in the city, however, no one is there to check whether this promise is fulfilled — or to note the long hours of drudgery, discrimination and isolation that are often the lot of these children.

Sinaga is the name of a town in western Kenya. To Christine and the other girls, the name has become synonymous with relief from the loneliness and neglect that characterize their

typical day. It is also a source of hope for the future.

Housed in a two-storey, white-painted concrete block building in Nairobi's industrial area, the NGO Sinaga offers basic education and training courses — including cooking classes — as well as comfort to young domestic workers. Barely two years old, its full title is Women and Child Labour Resource Centre, and it is funded by the International Labour Organization's International Programme to Eliminate Child Labour (ILO/IPEC).

Nearly 100 girls are currently enrolled in a six-month course that includes basic literacy, cooking, and introduction to skills such as tailoring and typing. The girls attend classes either in the morning or the afternoon, an arrangement negotiated with their employers by the Centre's field worker, Mary Musungu.

There is no charge to the employer. Ms. Musungu notes, "Once they realize that the child will get some education and that their work will still get done, they agree. But we have instances when girls are prevented from attending if they start to be too assertive, or question how they are treated in the home."

Few of the girls are assertive, though. "A child of 12 who's been labouring in a home since she was 7, cut off from contacts, often undernourished, bullied and abused by the woman employer, sometimes violated by the male, is usually very cowed," comments Sinaga's coordinator, Jane Ong'olo. The Centre, although functioning to an extent as a refuge for the girls, has as its main objective to equip them for the time when their usefulness to the employer is exhausted. Mrs. Ong'olo explains, "Very often these girls are pregnant at 14 or 15. Once that happens, they are put out on the streets, and their options for survival are extremely limited."

Having started out providing basic literacy for the youngest girls, and setting up the skills courses for the teenagers, Sinaga is finding that there is a demand for continuous service to assist the in-between-age girls. "We're not equipped to provide a school but the need is indicated. We would also like to offer counselling and legal advice for girls who are battered or abused. Sometimes they run away and come here — but we don't have the resources to act as a shelter," says Ms. Musungu.

As the sole centre of its kind in Kenya that offers both skills training and basic literacy to girls who are domestic workers, Sinaga has a ground-breaking role to play in sensitizing and informing the general public and authorities alike about conditions for domestic child workers and ways to improve them. Mrs. Ong'olo says, "This sort of work for children will not disappear overnight, but we can ensure that better conditions and working hours are mandatory."

Photo: Reaching child domestic workers with training and support programmes is a major challenge. A child in Uganda prepares a family's vegetables.

how many suffer physical or emotional damage, and to what degree, is even more hidden behind closed doors.[37]

Accurate information can be put to good use. In Kenya, for example, evidence of psychological and emotional damage has helped convince parents and society at large that the problem must be tackled (Panel 6). Both there and in Senegal, community drama projects have raised awareness, particularly in the rural areas likely to be the source of future domestic workers. A different approach has been taken in Sri Lanka, where the Government has targeted employers with large newspaper advertisements stressing that employing child domestics is illegal.[38]

Forced and bonded labour

Many of the forms of child labour practised around the world are 'forced' in the sense that children are taught to accept the conditions of their lives and not to challenge them.

But the situation of some children goes far beyond the acceptance of poor conditions. They find themselves in effective slavery. In South Asia, this has taken on a quasi-institutional form known as 'bonded' child labour. Under this system, children, often only eight or nine years old, are pledged by their parents to factory owners or their agents in exchange for small loans. Their lifelong servitude never succeeds in even reducing the debt.

In India, this type of transaction is widespread in agriculture, as well as in industries such as cigarette-rolling, carpet-making, matchstick-making, slate and silk. The most notorious of these is the carpet industry of Mirzapur-Bhadohi-Varanasi in Uttar Pradesh. According to a recent study, the thousands of children in the carpet industry are "kidnapped or lured away or pledged by their parents for paltry sums of money. Most of them are kept in captivity, tortured and made to work for 20 hours a day without a break. Little children are made to crouch on their toes, from dawn to dusk every day, severely stunting their growth during formative years. Social activists in the area find it hard to work because of the strong mafia-like control that the carpet loom owners have on the area."[39]

Of course, most worst-exploited children belong to the most marginalized segments of society. As in other countries, these ethnic minorities and disadvantaged groups are routinely seen as having no rights whatsoever. Often they themselves have come to believe that they deserve no rights.

This kind of virtual child slavery is usually associated only with India, Nepal and Pakistan. But it exists in other parts of the world, too. In Brazil, for example, forced labour is found from the charcoal-burning projects of Minas Gerais and Bahia to the sugar-cane estates of Espíritu Santo and the north-east. While most such labour is performed by adults, children are inevitably involved also. In 1993, a British Member of Parliament reported having seen children working to cool down charcoal kilns with mud in Açailândia.[40] Also in 1993, children as young as four were said to be at work in the cotton harvest in Paraná.[41] In Mauritania, thousands of children are still born each year into effective slavery. A tradition for generations, servitude was officially outlawed in 1980, but 400,000 black Africans serve as slaves, either formally or informally, to their Berber masters.[42] Another example is in Myanmar, where hundreds of thousands of people, including children, work on construction projects aimed at fostering tourism and economic expansion, often in appalling conditions.

In Nepal, children and women carry bricks on their heads from the brick field to a truck. They earn $0.25 for every 100 trips.

Village loan-sharks often act as procurers for city brothels, lending money to the family that the daughter's work must pay off.

Governments of countries where forced child labour exists must redouble their efforts to stamp out the practice and challenge the vested interests that so immorally maintain and benefit from it.

Commercial sexual exploitation

The underground nature of the multi-billion-dollar illegal industry in the commercial sexual exploitation of children makes it difficult to gather reliable data. But NGOs in the field estimate that each year at least 1 million girls worldwide are lured or forced into this form of hazardous labour, which can verge on slavery. Boys are also often exploited.

When scandals about child prostitution in developing countries break in the international media, it is usually a story about the phenomenon called sex tourism in which holiday-makers from the rich world, mainly, though not exclusively, men, travel to locations such as Brazil, the Dominican Republic, Thailand and elsewhere in search of sex with children.

But we should not lose sight of the fact that many thousands of young girls in numerous countries serve the sexual appetites of local men from all social and economic backgrounds. And widespread child prostitution exists in industrialized countries. In the US alone, at least 100,000 children are believed to be involved.

Direct links between the commercial sexual exploitation of children and other forms of exploitative labour are numerous. Notorious in their own right for appalling working conditions, Nepalese carpet factories, where 50 per cent of the workers are estimated to be children, are common sites of sexual exploitation by employers as well as recruitment centres for Indian brothels. Children are especially powerless to refuse abuse by employers, either as perpetrators or intermediaries.

Village loan-sharks often act as procurers for city brothels, lending money to the family that the daughter's work must pay off. However it happens, almost all such children are betrayed by those they trust and may end up trafficked long distances and across borders. Rescue and rehabilitation is complicated for children. They often end up being prosecuted by the very legal system that should be protecting them. Even if they make it home, perhaps having been deported as illegal immigrants, they may face stigma and rejection by their families and communities. Shunned, ignored and invisible, they often have little choice but to return to the brothel or the streets.

The physical and psychosocial damage inflicted by commercial sexual exploitation makes it one of the most hazardous forms of child labour. No matter how high the wages or how few the hours, the children involved have to confront serious health risks every day, including respiratory diseases, HIV and sexually transmitted diseases, unwanted pregnancies and drug addiction. But they are also plunged into a distorted reality in which violence and distrust, shame and rejection are the norms. "We have the same place that bums do in society," said a 15-year-old Senegalese girl exploited through prostitution. "No one wants to know us or be seen with us."

It is crucial that the international public should understand the layers of complicity that envelop this area of child exploitation. Although it is always easier and more comfortable to blame the exploiting 'pimps' or 'perverts' or even the victims themselves, no social sector can escape responsibility for the commercial sexual exploitation of children. Families — entrusted with the care, nurture and development of children — may be complicit in allowing the child's sexual exploitation. Research has consistently indicated that child abuse and incest are common precursors of the commercial sexual exploitation of children. Then, in addition to the people who actually buy sex, there are the traffickers, agents and intermediaries who profit from the sale of children. There are the professional criminals and syndicates that run brothels. There are the entrepreneurs who organize sex tours or who produce tourist brochures encouraging the notion that young girls or boys are sexually available. And there are all the people, including corrupt or apathetic officials, who look the other way.

Beyond even these actors are more elusive and impersonal influences that contribute to the child sex trade, such as a deeply rooted gender discrimination that blunts the perception of violence committed against girls. Global market forces have also contributed to the problem by widening the gap between rich and poor — encouraging migration, destabilizing families, destroying support systems and safety nets. Conflicts and wars, dozens of which are occurring around the world, also create conditions in which children are sexually exploited.

The problem is out in the open now, after decades of what has amounted to a cross-cultural conspiracy of silence. The World Congress against Commercial Sexual Exploitation of Children, held in Sweden in August 1996, put the issue on the world's agenda for the first time. The Agenda for Action agreed upon by participants will guide governments in developing programmes to address the problem.

Industrial and plantation work

"Children work on all types of jobs, such as carrying molten loams of glass stuck on the tips of iron rods, which are just two feet away from their bodies; drawing molten glass from tank furnaces in which the temperature is between 1,500 and 1,800 degrees centigrade and the arm is almost touching the furnace because the arm of a child is so small; joining and annealing the glass bangles where the work is done over a small kerosene flame in a room with little or no ventilation because a whiff of air can blow out the flame. The whole factory floor is strewn with broken glass and the children run to and fro carrying this burning hot glass with no shoes to protect their feet. Naked electric wires are to be seen dangling everywhere because the factory owners could not be bothered to install insulated internal wiring." This is a description of the glass-bangle industry in Firozabad (India), in which one quarter of the workforce — around 50,000 — are children under 14.[43]

All over the world, children work in hazardous conditions. The industries are manifold, from leather-working in the Naples region of Italy to the pre-industrial brick-making of Colombia and Peru, which can involve children as young as eight.

Children are sometimes exploited in mining operations that would be considered too risky for adults in the industrialized world — for example, in the diamond and gold mines of Côte d'Ivoire and South Africa, and in Colombian coal mines. Typically, the children work with the barest minimum of safety equipment and constantly breathe in coal dust.

The respiratory problems faced by child miners are also common in other industries. Many suffer from tuberculosis, bronchitis and asthma. Children working in earthenware and porcelain factories, for example, are often unprotected from the silica dust. In the lock industry, they inhale noxious

Nearly a third of the agricultural workforce in some developing countries is made up of children, according to a recent ILO report. This young cane cutter is one of millions of children under the age of 14 working in Brazil.

Iolanda Huzak

37

Agricultural labour: A harsh harvest

UNICEF/96-0461/Balaguer

From a distance, the scene has a bucolic beauty, with deep green tea plants massed against the hillside and figures moving slowly through the rows. The sun is barely up, and the early morning mist clings low on the ground. Distance, however, masks reality.

Those who pick the tea or coffee — or cut cane or sisal, or harvest rubber and cocoa — know the harshness of agricultural work firsthand. The backbone of countless societies is backbreaking labour, done with little help from mechanization, under gruelling conditions. And in this planting and plucking, hoeing and raking, children play a large — and largely invisible — role.

No comprehensive data exist on how many children work the world's fields. But a recent report from the International Labour Organization (ILO) says that in some developing countries, nearly a third of the agricultural workforce is comprised of children. Only relatively recently have specific ILO country studies shown how much children contribute to

world food and agricultural commodity production.

In Bangladesh, fully 82 per cent of the country's 6.1 million economically active children work in agriculture, according to a 1989 survey. As many as 3 million children, age 10 to 14, are estimated to work in Brazil's sisal, tea, sugar-cane and tobacco plantations.

In Turkey, a 1989 study found that 60 per cent of workers involved in cotton cultivation were 20 years old or younger. Children are believed to comprise one fourth of all agricultural workers in Kenya. And a 1993 study in Malawi found that the majority of children living on tobacco estates were working full- or part-time (78 per cent of 10- to 14-year-olds and 55 per cent of 7- to 9-year-olds). The situation is by no means restricted to the developing world. Entire families of migrant labourers, including children, help plant and harvest the industrialized world's fruits and vegetables.

The risks are multiple. Children pick crops still dripping with pesticides or spray the chemicals themselves. They

face poisonous snakes and insects and cut themselves on tough stems and on the tools they use. Rising early to work in the damp and cold, often barefoot and dressed in inadequate clothes, they develop chronic coughs and pneumonia. The hours in the fields are long — 8- to 10-hour days are not uncommon — and spent far from running water or other simple comforts.

Skin, eye, respiratory or neurological problems occur in children exposed to agrochemicals or involved in processing crops like sisal. Children harvesting tobacco in Tanzania experience the nausea, vomiting and faintness of nicotine poisoning. Frequent heavy lifting and repetitive strains can permanently injure growing spines. And fatigue plagues those lucky enough to attend school after their work.

Because children have traditionally helped on family farms and in fields, legislation designed to protect children from damaging work — in factories, mines and other industries — usually does not apply to agriculture, making agricultural workers among the least protected of all.

But such work has always had the potential to harm children's development. Some societies make provisions for children's help in the fields — long summer holidays in the northern hemisphere for instance, so children's school work doesn't suffer. Many others do not.

And commercial agriculture — removed from sight, on remote farmlands and plantations and with its quotas, high use of chemicals and profit pressures — has more in common with industrial sweatshops than with an ideal family farm.

Legal, social, economic and educational initiatives are all needed to protect children from the dangers they face, especially since agricultural workers are among the world's poorest.

The Child Welfare Association of Thailand, in collaboration with the country's Ministry of Agriculture and

Cooperatives, studied child workers in sugar-cane and rubber plantations and proposed that the same labour laws for the industrial sector be applied, with appropriate exceptions, to the agricultural sector. They recommended that laws provide for: minimum age for workers because of hazardous working conditions; written employment contracts; and days off and paid leave for all workers. A minimum wage rate of at least 80 per cent of the adult minimum wage was urged for children who had reached the age of legal employment. To ensure compliance with the legal provisions, a special government body should oversee a trained inspectorate, with exclusive responsibility for child agricultural labour.

The study also recommended that public education campaigns be conducted and that government officials, NGO workers, employers, children and their families be made thoroughly familiar with the meaning and ramifications of child labour laws. Greater educational opportunities and skills training were also called for.

Children who live in poor, rural communities face the greatest risks from hazardous and exploitative agricultural labour. Improving the infrastructure of rural areas through better roads and power supplies can boost agricultural productivity and help protect the rights of children and families. Broader family participation in credit and income-enhancing schemes are other invaluable measures.

Photo: Commercial agriculture with its quotas, use of chemicals and profit pressures has more in common with industrial sweatshops than with an ideal family farm. A child in Peru helps carry grasses.

fumes given off by dangerous chemicals. In the brassware industry, children work at high-temperature furnaces and inhale the dust produced in polishing.[44]

The numbers of children exploited by plantation agriculture across the world may be just as great — and the dangers associated with much of their work are no less appalling (Panel 7). In Brazil's sugar plantations, for example, children cut cane with machetes, a punishing task putting them at constant risk of mutilation. They make up a third of the workforce in some areas and are involved in over 40 per cent of the work-related accidents. Brazilian children are also exposed to snakebites and insect stings on tobacco plantations, and carry loads far beyond their capacities. In Colombia, young people who work on flower-export farms are exposed to pesticides banned in industrialized countries.

In Africa, meanwhile, children work on the plantations that grow the export crops on which the continent's economies rely — from the cocoa and coffee estates of Côte d'Ivoire to the tea, coffee and sisal plantations of Tanzania. In Zimbabwe, children work a 60-hour week picking cotton or coffee for about $1. An ILO study on child labour in Zimbabwe found that the most significant exploiters of child labour seemed to be the large-scale commercial farmers who have used children in their fields for decades, especially during planting and harvesting.[45] These commercial farmers campaigned against the Government's draft child labour regulations in 1995, on the grounds that they would interfere with children's right to work. The same year, farmers asked a District Education Officer to close down the schools to allow children to help bring in the tea and coffee crops. The request, which was

In the brassware industry, children work at high-temperature furnaces and inhale the dust produced in polishing.

The numbers of children working on the streets have grown in recent years in certain areas. A girl sells brown sugar cones on a city street in Egypt.

UNICEF/96-0262/Toutounji

reported in the local press, was turned down.

In Indonesia, children — most of them girls — work on tobacco plantations for $0.60 a day, well below the legal minimum wage.[46] In Nepal, children work on tea estates for wages so low that they often need to work 14 hours a day. Children are also employed on the tea plantations of Bangladesh, India and Sri Lanka,[47] while child labourers in the sugarcane and rubber plantations of Thailand are at constant risk of injury from dangerous equipment.[48]

While much of this industrial and plantation work is carried out by national subcontractors, some of it is overseen by transnational corporations whose products find their way into the ordinary stores and homes of the West. The *maquiladoras* (assembly plants) of Central America and Mexico are a case in point. Large corporations based in rich countries have transferred their assembly functions to poorer countries to take advantage of their lower wage and benefit costs. In a much publicized case in Honduras, for example, 12- and 13-year-old girls working for a US-based transnational were locked inside a textile factory. Hours were long, wages pitiable, the temperature hit 100 degrees Fahrenheit and there was no safe drinking water.[49]

Such cases have led activists both in the home and the host countries of these transnationals to pressure them to establish codes of conduct not only for their operations but also for those of the subcontractors they use. All corporations should adopt such codes of conduct as an essential step towards eliminating hazardous child labour.

But most child labour in the formal economy cannot be tied so directly to the operation of transnationals. This is why national as well as transnational companies need to adopt codes of conduct that bar hazardous child labour.

Street work

In contrast with child domestic workers, some children work in the most visible places possible — on the streets of developing world cities and towns (Panel 8). They are everywhere: hawking in markets and darting in and out of traffic jams, plying their trade at bus and train stations, in front of hotels and shopping malls. They share the streets with millions of adults, many of whom regard them as nuisances, if not as dangerous mini-criminals. What most of these children actually do on the streets is, of course, work.

The street is a cruel and hazardous workplace, often jeopardizing even children's lives. They can be murdered by organized crime, by other young people or even by the police. The world reacted in horror in 1993 when Rio de Janeiro police officers massacred six street children. In 1996, a Rio police officer confessed and became the first-ever police officer to be convicted of the murder of street children. But the killings of street youth had already started in Rio by 1990. A report from the state juvenile court stated that, on average, three street children are killed every day in Rio, many by police at the request of merchants who consider the begging, thieving and glue-sniffing a major nuisance.[50]

Many children do pursue these activities. But many more struggle at legitimate work on the street for their own or their family's survival. Children who work on the streets often come from slums and squatter settlements, where poverty and precarious family situations are common, where schools are overcrowded and poor, and where safe places to play simply do not exist. Their numbers have increased in places experiencing armed conflict, like Freetown (Sierra Leone) and Monrovia (Liberia), as caretakers have been killed, the economy disrupted and family and community ties severed.

Street child labour, virtually unheard of prior to the transition to a market economy, is now a growing problem in the Russian Federation. In Kyrgyzstan, in Central Asia, the numbers of children working on the streets, selling food and other products, have increased dramatically over the last three years. Many have dropped out of school or never attended classes.

On the streets, they shine shoes, wash and guard cars, carry luggage, hawk flowers and trinkets, collect recyclables and find a myriad other ingenious ways to make money. The amount they earn may be small but is sometimes more than they would receive from formal-sector work.

The large majority of these children return home each night. They are children on the streets, not of them. Still, life is often precarious and violent, unhealthy and unfair. Some are able to combine some schooling with their street work, but nevertheless many are exploited and cheated by adults and peers and must spend many hours earning their survival. Many suffer from malnutrition and from illnesses including tuberculosis. Self-esteem is often low, despite the superficial air of exaggerated self-confidence they may assume to appear street-smart.

For about 1 in 10, the street does become home. Inevitably these children become more prone to engage in marginal and illegal work, such as begging and petty thieving. Many are led into the illicit, thrilling and dangerous world of crime syndicates that run rings for pickpocketing, burglary, drug trafficking and prostitution. The subculture that envelops the lives of these children is marked by aggression and abuse, exposing them to extreme hazards.

Scavenging is one example of the extreme risks children face in street work. In cities across the developing world, young children spend their days picking up used paper, plastics, rags, bottles, tin and metal pieces from the street, garbage dumps and waste bins, and selling them to retailers for recycling.

"The nature of their work is… most unhygienic, dangerous, demeaning…. They develop several kinds of skin disease like ulcers, scabies, etc. While collecting rusted iron pieces, they usually receive cuts on their hands and become susceptible to tetanus. The broken glass lying hidden in the garbage may injure their bare feet, which may develop into festering wounds. Many other sicknesses arise from exposure to extreme weather conditions, like cases of sunstroke, pneumonia, influenza and malaria. Carrying heavy loads under the arms or on their back adversely affects the height, weight, strength and stamina. Added to these hazards is the lure of eating thrown away or leftover food…[leading] to digestive disorders and food poisoning."[51]

Attempts are being made in many countries to wean children off the streets and to protect them while they are on the streets. One inspiring example of action is in Brazil, long a country identified with the 'problem' of street children. The National Children's Movement — a partnership between the children and voluntary 'educators', themselves from poor backgrounds — was established in 1985, and its first meeting in 1986 caused a national sensation, helping to enshrine child rights in the fledgling democracy. Each of its national

Most children working on the street struggle at legitimate jobs for their own or their family's survival. In Tanzania, a boy washes cars.

The streets are their workplace

UNICEF/96-0046/Charton

Ten-year-old Shireen, a professional scavenger, has never been to school. But she is well versed in the economics of survival: if she sells 30 to 50 cents' worth of waste paper and plastic bags, she eats lunch; if she earns less, she goes without food. Such is the cruel but practical calculus of work and life on the streets.

Shireen is one of hundreds of thousands of children who work day to day on city streets, sometimes making their homes there as well. Whether raking through garbage dumps, shining shoes outside hotels or begging at busy intersections, they are living barometers of societies in stress. Largely found in the developing world — but also in affluent countries — children working on the streets are the progeny of some of the most disturbing social phenomena in the world today: rapid urban-

ization, runaway population growth and increasing disparities in wealth. Their rising numbers also indicate a constellation of other trends, such as cut-backs in government social and educational budgets, as well as the breakdown of traditional family and community structures, which leaves children unprotected.

In Zaire, they are called *moineaux* or 'sparrows'. In Peru, *pájaros fruteros* or 'fruitbirds'. But everywhere, children working on the streets are scorned, mistreated and misunderstood. "People don't love us," says Tigiste, a 12-year-old girl, who sells roasted barley and begs for change at stop lights in the Ethiopian capital of Addis Ababa.

Often fleeing abuse and neglect at home, children find further abuse and exploitation on the street. In many cases, without legal identity, they are

manipulated by organized crime, street gangs, pimps and unscrupulous employers, sometimes dealing drugs or working in prostitution. In the words of Josie, 10, who has been selling candy on Manila thoroughfares since she was four: "Every day I pray not to end up in evil hands."

Less commonly known is the finding that children who work the streets provide critical financial support for their families, as well as paying for their own education when they can. Their hallmarks are ingenuity, practical intelligence and a relentless will to survive — whether that means hunting scraps of metal for the mattress-makers in the markets of Dakar, or, as in the Philippines, praying in churches on behalf of customers.

In a striking contrast to the largely throw-away cultures of the industrialized world, in the developing world, many children subsist as waste-heap recyclers. Plastic bags, blown-out tyres, junked car parts, empty bottles and tins, even scrap paper — all are collected diligently by children who scour the urban landscape. Pre-teens in the Philippines comb city streets, collecting everything from bronze wire to old newspapers. In a country where the per capita gross national product (GNP) is about $900, these children earn up to $3 a day from their scavenging, supplying their families with necessities like rice, firewood, gas and mosquito repellent. Similarly, six hours on Manila's immense 'Smoky Mountain' garbage dump can earn a child more than an adult earns for a 10-hour shift at a nearby factory.

Regardless of what it can pay, though, scavenging is hazardous work, also considered so degrading by the children themselves that many quit, even turning to prostitution. "The nature of their work and work environment is most unhygienic, dangerous, demeaning and destructive of self-worth," writes one social scientist who has studied the rag-pickers of Bangalore (India). Tramping through garbage heaps in every kind of weather exposes children to skin infections, tetanus and other diseases. Back-breaking loads stunt growth, and eating discarded food often brings sickness. Furthermore, the life of trash collecting offers no hope for a better future.

Organizations like Reach Up in the Philippines and the Bosco Yuvodaya Street Children Project of Bangalore have begun helping children to band together and collectively defend their interests. Opportunities for formal and non-formal education and apprenticeship training, such as those offered by Uganda's Africa Foundation and the Undugu Society of Kenya, offer hope for a better future.

Children living on the street, without homes or families, pose the greatest challenge in terms of rehabilitation, often needing long-term one-on-one counselling. Preventive measures are, therefore, vital to protect children from the risk of full exposure to life on the street.

Photo: At a large refuse dump in Cambodia, a girl collects waste she can sell for recycling.

congresses — the fourth was held in 1995 — has heralded a new advance in thinking about children's problems. Just as important, the Movement bases its organization on small groups (*nucleos de base*) of working children who meet to discuss common problems and to take joint action. This model of organization seeks to empower children. "What would I do if there was no *nucleo de base*?" an 11-year-old delegate to last year's congress responded to a reporter. "I would go right out and start one."[52]

Work for the family

Of all the work children do, the most common is agricultural or domestic work within their own families. Most families around the world expect their children to help in the household, whether preparing food, fetching water or groceries, herding animals, caring for younger siblings or more arduous work in the fields. This kind of work can be beneficial. Children learn from a reasonable level of participation in household chores, subsistence food-growing and income-generating activities. They also derive a sense of self-worth from their work within their families.

But it is by no means always beneficial. On the contrary, work for the family may demand too much of children, requiring them to labour long hours that keep them from school and take too great a toll on their developing bodies (Panel 9). Such work can prevent children from exercising their rights and developing to their full potential.

One powerful testimony to the rigours of work in the rural home comes from a group of Nepalese children now working in a Kathmandu carpet factory. They were attracted by stories of the excitement of the city and by the idea of earning wages both for themselves and to send back to

Of all the work children do, the most common is agricultural or domestic work within their own families.

Girls and women routinely bear burdens and endure treatment that reflect their unequal status. Working girls are often invisible, treated as if they did not exist.

their parents. But most of all, they said, they had come to the factory because life at home was so difficult: climbing up steep slopes to get fodder, risking leeches; having to labour endlessly to feed the family.[53] To avoid these lives, they had ended up in carpet-making, an industry notorious for its exploitation.

In rural Africa and in South Asia, children begin helping with domestic chores well before school age. Girls must fetch the household's water and fuelwood. Children of both sexes help with farm work, looking after animals and performing all tasks to do with water, jobs often physically taxing in the extreme. They also work in the informal sector of the rural economy, including traditional crafts and small trades essential to village life, especially shopkeeping.

Similar patterns of early labour are reported in a survey of five Latin American countries.[54] In rural Colombia, for instance, one in four children aged 6 to 9 and one in three aged 10 and 11 work, either in the home, tending the family vegetable garden, caring for animals, or helping in a grocery store or small business. In the country's large cities, one in six of 10- and 11-year-old children and one in ten of 6- to 9-year-olds participate in the labour market in some way.

Much of this work, particularly by girls within their homes, is invisible to the statistician aiming to measure the scale of child labour. It is also excluded from child labour legislation, partly because of the difficulty of policing child labour within the family. Yet to accept that such work cannot be regulated is to accept that hundreds of millions of children can have no legal protection.

Legislation must be made more inclusive, but this will not of itself protect these children. The difficulties of enforcement will remain. But at the

very least it will spread the message that there are strict limits as to what can be expected of a child's labour in the home. It may also make affirmative action more possible, and open social discussions involving parents and community members on what is considered to be good for a child.

Girls' work

"Nearly all our girls work as sweepers," says a mother from India, herself a sweeper or latrine-cleaner. "Why should I waste my time and money on sending my daughter to school where she will learn nothing of use?… So why not put my girl to work so that she will learn something about our profession? My elder girl who is 15 years old will be married soon. Her mother-in-law will put her to cleaning latrines somewhere. Too much schooling will only give girls big ideas, and then they will be beaten up by their husbands or abused by their in-laws."[55]

Most of the hazards faced by boy labourers are faced by girls, too. Yet girls have extra problems of their own: from the sexual pressures of employers to exclusion from education. No strategy to combat child labour can begin to be successful unless these special dangers facing girls are systematically taken into account.

In virtually every area of life and in every country, as these annual *State of the World's Children* reports have long noted, girls and women routinely bear burdens and endure treatment that reflect their unequal status. So it is with child labour. Working girls are often invisible, treated as if they did not exist.

According to ILO, 56 per cent of the 10- to 14-year-olds currently estimated to be working in the developing world are boys. Yet, if we were able to measure the numbers of girls doing unregistered work as domestic help, or working at home to enable other family members to take up paid employment, the figures would show more female child labourers than male. Girls also work longer hours on average than boys, carrying a double workload — a job outside the home and domestic duties on their return.

In Guatemala, working girls spend an average of 21 hours a week on household duties on top of a 40-hour working week outside. And in five Latin American countries surveyed, domestic work by girls in their own home was widespread, with many failing to attend school.[56]

All over the world, more girls than boys are denied their fundamental right to primary schooling. In some regions, including the Middle East and North Africa, sub-Saharan Africa and especially South Asia, the gender gap is still enormous.[57] Educational equality between the sexes is being approached in East Asia and Latin America and the Caribbean, but elsewhere little progress has been recorded.

Gender bias is not simply a question of attitudes — it is enshrined in all the main institutions of society. Nepal illustrates the point only too well. Women's socio-economic status is often deplorable. And while the proportion of men who can read and write — 37 per cent — is extremely low, the 11 per cent figure for female literacy is appalling.[58] The overwhelming majority of girls either have never gone to school or have dropped out to work. Discrimination soon becomes exploitation. Lack of education, early arranged marriages, stark poverty and lack of power make girls enormously vulnerable. Long before they are physically prepared for it, many are forced to work, most of them ending up, if not in domestic service then in the carpet industry, on tea estates or in brick-making.

The gender gap becomes a vicious circle for girls all over the developing world. Unable to attend school because of their low social status or their domestic responsibilities, they are denied the extra power and wider horizons that education would bring. If they seek work outside the home, their opportunities are limited to the most menial tasks. Their low status is reinforced and passed on to the next generation.

Both the individual and the society suffer. It is well established that the more schooling a girl has, the fewer children she will bear. The more children a poor family has, the more child workers there will be.[59]

Two young girls threshing rice in Indonesia.

UNICEF/1860/Sprague

Ideas and actions

Intolerable forms of child labour are so grave an abuse of human rights that the world must come to regard them in the way it does slavery — as something unjustifiable under any circumstances.

While legislation and acts of ratification are important first steps, the lives of working children will not change unless the world backs its words with action. As this report has already made clear, the Convention on the Rights of the Child, the most widely ratified human rights agreement in the history of the United Nations, holds special promise in this regard, binding ratifying countries to take concrete actions to uphold it.

Less than a year after the Convention was adopted, the World Summit for Children was held at the United Nations on 29-30 September 1990. It was the largest ever gathering of world leaders till that time. The 159 countries represented — 71 of them by Heads of State or Government — strongly endorsed the Convention. They jointly signed a World Declaration on the Survival, Protection and Development of Children and a Plan of Action for implementing the Declaration in the 1990s.

The Declaration is not a legally binding document, but its moral force is clear. The world's leaders agreed to be guided by the principle that the essential needs of children should be given high priority in the allocation of resources in bad times as well as good. They affirmed that all children must be given the chance to "realize their worth in a safe and supportive environment..."[60] They vowed: "We ourselves hereby make a solemn commitment to give high priority to the rights of children, to their survival and to their protection and development."[61] Moreover, they made an explicit pledge: "We will work for special protection of the working child and for the abolition of illegal child labour."[62]

The Plan of Action, meanwhile, includes the following statement: "More than 100 million children are engaged in employment, often heavy and hazardous and in contravention of international conventions which provide for their protection from economic exploitation and from performing work that interferes with their education and is harmful to their health and full development. With this in mind, all States should work to end such child labour practices and see how the conditions and circumstances of children in legitimate employment can be protected to provide adequate opportunity for their healthy upbringing and development."[63]

The voice of the world is firm and crystal clear. There is no ambiguity or equivocation here. ILO efforts to establish a new international convention on the elimination of hazardous child labour is another example of continuing global commitment and has UNICEF's full support.

Yet ending hazardous child labour and protecting children are not as easy as saying you will do so. In addition, there are different opinions among those working to end hazardous child labour on how best to proceed. Some believe that labour that is damaging to children has to be treated like slavery: it is an abuse of *civil and political* human rights so fundamental that it must simply be outlawed without compromise. Others see hazardous child labour as primarily an abuse of *social and economic* human rights. While just as committed to its eradication in the long term, they are immediately concerned about protecting children at work, rather than liberating them into conceivably more difficult circumstances.

Coherent programmes to combat hazardous and exploitative child labour will have to draw from the expertise and experience of both camps. Intolerable forms of child labour are so grave an abuse of human rights that the world must come to regard them in the way it does slavery — as something unjustifiable under any circumstances. The international community must invest in public education campaigns that drive home the message that hazardous child labour will be as unacceptable in the next century as slavery has become in this.

Yet it is equally clear that any programme of elimination that does not provide reasonable alternatives for child workers — which from high moral ground simply casts them out of a workplace they had only entered due to extreme poverty — would trigger an avalanche of negative consequences.

Any comprehensive attack on hazardous child labour must advance on several fronts. It must aim to: release children immediately from the most damaging situations, such as bonded labour and prostitution; rehabilitate those children who are released from work through the provision of adequate services and facilities, especially education; and protect working children who cannot immediately be released, making their life as safe and as conducive to development as possible.

But the most important front of all is prevention: ensuring that new generations of children are not driven into the most hazardous forms of work.

There is a vast range of ideas about how to tackle unacceptable forms of child labour, and a large and growing body of experience. The problem is so huge and diverse that multiple strategies are needed. Since the 1990 World Summit, over 150 industrialized and developing nations have drawn up national programmes of action for meeting the World Summit goals. Countries need to review their national programmes to ensure that they include provisions on child labour and protection of children from hazardous and exploitative labour.

Any comprehensive attack on child labour must also mobilize a wide range of protagonists: governments and local communities, NGOs and spiritual leaders, employers and trade unions, the child labourers themselves and their families.

Schoolchildren parade through their community to announce Peru's national immunization programme beginning the following day.

Some will be more motivated by protecting the children involved; others by enhancing the educational opportunities that provide a way out of the cycle of child labour and poverty; and still others by helping raise global awareness of this fundamental abuse of human rights. The important point is not that one particular strategy dominates but that maximum energy and attention are applied to the problem.

Reliable and comparable data on the extent and nature of child labour are a key element in the effort to eliminate the problem, and effective solutions cannot be fashioned without such information. Governments, communities, NGOs and UN agencies must together create a system of data collection that will quantify the numbers of children now labouring in hazardous and exploitative conditions — whether on plantations, as domestic workers, on the streets, in sweatshops or in factories — and document the conditions of their labour. In this context, the participatory learning and action techniques, involving community members in assessing and devising solutions to the child labour problem in the glass industry of Firozabad (India), are proving particularly valuable.

Most key initiatives being taken fall into one of five categories: promoting and enhancing the education alternative; building on national and international legislation and improving enforcement; empowering the poor; mobilizing all levels of society to combat the exploitative forms of child labour; and campaigning to persuade corporations to show greater responsibility for their actions and those of their subcontractors.

The power of education

A comprehensive strategy to combat hazardous child labour must begin with its logical alternative: high-quality schools and relevant educational programmes to which families will want to send their children and in which children will want to participate.

There are 140 million children between the ages of 6 and 11 not attending school — 23 per cent of primary school age children in developing countries — and perhaps an equal number who drop out of school early (Fig. 7). If all those under 18 are considered to be children, as the Convention on the Rights of the Child stipulates, the figure out of school rises to 404 million, or 38 per cent of that age group.[64] Many of these children work, many in jobs that are disabling and dangerous. Millions more are trying hard to balance the demands of work and schooling, a juggling act that poses particular problems for girls.

ILO, reflecting a broad consensus, takes the position that the single most effective way to stem the flow of school age children into abusive forms of employment or work is to extend and improve schooling so that it will attract and retain them.[65]

Education and child labour interact profoundly. As we have seen, work can keep children away from school. At the same time, poor-quality education often causes children to drop out of school and start working at an early age. Good-quality education, on the other hand, can keep children away from work. The longer and better the education, the lesser the likelihood that a child will be forced into damaging work.

The Convention on the Rights of the Child insists that primary education must be universal and compulsory. If governments delivered on their legal commitment to this, the extent of exploitative child labour would be significantly reduced. The

A boy mechanic at work in a street stall in Nepal.

UNICEF/93-1274/Murray-Lee

"How can I study?"

In the opinion of many people, all children should be in school until they are 15 or 16 years old. But what if the schools are very few, and very poorly equipped? And what if many families are so poor that even the small amounts earned by children are essential to pay for the basic necessities of living? What about children who have lost one or both parents? With whom do they live? Even where non-governmental and other organizations have established schools in low-income residential areas, there are distressing numbers of children who simply cannot afford to go to them. Others seemingly want to work, or at least feel mature doing the same work as adults.

Education planners frequently ask the question: "Do working children really want to go to school?" Recent interviews with working children in Bangladesh conclude that the large majority do want to attend school and have clear ideas about the value of education, as the following synopses show.

Taslima, age 13, began working in a garment factory when she was 9 years old. Now she would like very much to go to school to study Bangla, maths and English. If school expenses were provided, she says, it would be possible to attend classes in the morning and work in the afternoon. When asked about the benefit of education, she says that she will learn to count and write letters. She would also like to learn music and sewing.

Shujon, age 8, came to Dhaka with his mother, brother and grandmother in search of a living. His mother works as a domestic servant and earns 100 taka (1 taka is about $0.02) per month. Shujon and his brother collect plastic bags, scrap paper and other materials, which they sell at a shop for 5 to 10 taka per bagful. The boys attend a free school near the railway station. They go there every day for several hours and are taught to read and write. The school gives them a snack of roti and banana every day and all the necessary books and writing supplies.

Rakib is 10 years old and is now attending school after he lost his job at a garment factory for being under age. Rakib wants to study. He says, "If I study, I'll get a good job. I will be able to help my mother."

Amina began working to earn money at the age of 7, collecting waste paper. Now 10, she spends her days breaking bricks into small pieces for construction projects in Dhaka. Amina is very small. She cannot break many bricks. She does not know how much she earns, as her mother keeps track of those things. Sometimes they decide to collect scrap paper instead, because their hands and fingers hurt from the gashes and blows that happen when the bricks break in unexpected ways, or the hammer slips in their hands. Amina would like to find out what school is like, if only there were some way to pay even the minimal costs.

Shilpi is a 14-year-old garment worker from Mirpur. She found a job as a helper in a garment factory. She folds the shirts that are produced by machine operators. Her salary is 400 taka per month. She says she would like to study but that earning a living is the first priority, "I have to take care of myself. How can I study?" When asked about her future, she says she wants to be a teacher. She loves to see teachers teaching others. She taught her younger brother to read, she says.

Julekha is 13 years old and has been a domestic worker from the age of 10. Her father is paralysed and cannot work. She has three sisters and four brothers. Her main duty is to look after the employer's small child, but she also assists in all household chores. If the family goes out, Julekha is locked in the house. Julekha has never attended school because of her family's poverty, but says she would like to if it were possible.

Ruma, age 12, wants to study. She thinks if she received an education she would be able to help her parents and give them advice. And, she says, "when talk of marriage is going on, I will have something to say." She would like to learn how to operate a sewing machine. Then her salary would increase, and everybody would suffer less. She hopes she will be able to study while continuing to work.

— Adapted from *Daily Lives of Working Children in Bangladesh: Case studies*, by P. Pelto, UNICEF Bangladesh, (unpublished).

Non-formal education:
A bridge for working children

UNICEF/ESARO/Pirozzi

When hardship forced Sadhan Sarkar's ageing parents to pull him out of school and put him to work long hours in a shop, the seven-year-old boy cried bitterly. "I was angry — at my work, my boss, my parents," he recalls. Then, field workers for the Balia Gram Unnayan Samity project (BGUS), in India's West Bengal state, intervened and convinced his parents to let Sadhan quit work and resume his studies. Now third in his primary school class, he says, "I have a new life, I can laugh and play and read again."

Sadhan is one of hundreds of at-risk working children helped since 1993 by BGUS, a non-governmental organization (NGO) in Tarakeshwar affiliated with the Christian Children's Fund. Through a support system that provides school supplies, health services and a midday meal, BGUS estimates that 370 children have been able to quit work and continue their education, while another 19 children over age 14 have obtained skilled jobs through vocational training.

Scores of organizations similar to BGUS have sprung up in recent years,

responding to the needs of the world's child labourers. Education, essential in ensuring better opportunities for child workers, is a common thread throughout these programmes. The challenge is to make schooling economically viable, attractive and relevant for working children and their families.

Methods used to pursue this goal vary. As Victor Ordoñez of UNESCO says: "Do we try and use non-formal education to get children back into the regular school system, or teach them what they need to survive day to day?" Like BGUS, many programmes aim for community-based, sustainable alternatives that have elements of both, providing working children with education and health care.

A two-year-old programme for children released from Nepal's carpet factories, operated by the Underprivileged Children's Education Programme and the Asian-American Free Labor Institute, offers free food, lodging and a mix of formal and non-formal education. Its self-described role is as "a way station to somewhere else — hopefully a better life," whether enrolment in school or a

job using new vocational skills. Brazil's widely acclaimed Projeto Axé offers primary school age children remedial classes to help them enter the formal system. It also works with teenagers, teaching everything from dance and printing techniques to remedial education, to provide "a transition from a street past to a citizen present." CREDA, an NGO in India's Uttar Pradesh state, has opened 60 schools for former bonded labourers that compress five years of basic education into three.

Other projects focus on improving young workers' basic literacy or training them for a new trade altogether. The Undugu Society of Kenya, for example, runs five schools for children who earn their living collecting scrap. The schools operate half-days to accommodate work schedules, and classes emphasize numeracy to enable children to avoid exploitation by scrap dealers.

In Senegal, the ENDA-Tiers Monde organization teamed up with the Ministry for Social Development in 1984 to improve the self-esteem of teenage girls working as domestics, as well as giving them professional opportunities. The programme includes basic literacy and vocational training to raise their chances of obtaining better jobs, as well as counselling on health matters including AIDS.

A common problem in dealing with working children is how to keep the poorest, whose income is most critical to their own or their family's survival, in school. Relevant curricula, flexible class schedules and quality education are essential. Scholarships and other ways of covering the direct costs of schooling, as well as cash stipends to compensate families for 'lost' income, form important parts of several programmes.

At schools opened by the Bangladesh Independent Garment Workers Union, for example, children who lost jobs in the apparel industry receive free books and hot lunches. In Honduras, more than 2,000 young street workers have benefited from formal and non-formal education at Project Alternatives & Opportunities, which provides health care, counselling, school supplies, uniforms and, when needed, partial scholarships and nutritional supplements. Fundación CISOL, in Loja (Ecuador), pays weekly stipends that approximate the earnings of a shoeshine boy, while teaching handicraft production. Participating children must resume regular schooling.

Cash stipends are considered controversial by some experts who think they encourage dependency; others insist that stipends are the only way many families can afford to educate their children.

An innovative programme implemented by the Federal District of Brazil pays an education grant equal to the minimum wage to poor families whose children do not miss more than two days of school per month. The School Savings Programme, which also includes a savings and credit plan, has dramatically lowered the drop-out rate among poor students. It is also affordable, accounting for less than 1 per cent of the annual government budget.

Such programmes point to growing efforts by governments to ensure primary education to all children — including child labourers. Governments, together with NGOs, industries and workers' organizations, are forming the social partnerships that are necessary to address the problems of working children.

Photo: In a non-formal education programme, a Kenyan girl learns carpentry.

resources to create good schools all over the world could be found if the will was there. What is more, innovative thinking about how to regenerate the education system is well under way, and successful programmes exist all over the world that could serve as models.

Any improvement made to education — whether by changing existing schools, by setting up creative and flexible approaches to education or by targeting working children specifically — will have a positive impact on child labour. The more we do, the greater will be the results. What more powerful incentive could there be?

Improving basic education

The 1990 World Conference on Education for All, held in Jomtien (Thailand), proclaimed the need for diverse, flexible approaches within a unified national system of primary education. To achieve the goal of quality primary education for all, education systems must:

► *Teach useful skills*. If schools are to attract and retain children, their courses have to be seen as relevant by both parents and children (Panel 10). One prerequisite of a successful state education programme is that it links the lessons taught to community life. In places where most children work, it defies logic to continue teaching as if they do not. Children must be taught which kinds of work are particularly hazardous and be advised on how to recognize the tactics of exploitative employers.

Children also need to be taught general life skills and about their own rights, so that they understand child labour laws and what they mean in practice. "In school they do not teach us about our rights," says Lakshmi, from Kolkere in southern India. "We cannot wait until later to

Any improvement made to education — whether by changing existing schools, by setting up creative and flexible approaches to education or by targeting working children specifically — will have a positive impact on child labour.

51

Fig. 7 Children out of school: A cost and a cause of child labour

How the regions compare

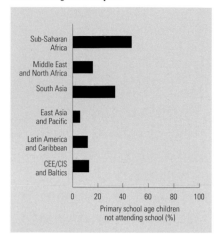

The global picture

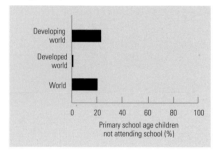

Source: UNICEF data.

learn about them. To protect ourselves, we need that information right now."[66]

▶ *Be more flexible*. Schools have to adapt to children's circumstances. The annual calendar and daily timetable of a school can be adjusted according to the seasonal farming calendar in the area. This has been one of the strategies adopted by the Indian state of Kerala, where very low school drop-out rates are matched by low incidence of child labour.

Schools also have to move towards children, particularly in rural areas. Small multigrade classes can bring education within easy walking distance. A simplified curriculum and locally produced learning materials can ensure that the basics are available to all; the programme can be enriched gradually over time. Teachers with modest formal education have proven to be effective when given concentrated practical training and frequent in-service upgrades.

Most important, rigid traditional teaching methods must give way to child-centred approaches. Children must enjoy education if it is to have a powerful effect.

The Escuela Nueva programme in Colombia exemplifies many of these flexible approaches. This successful programme, bringing education to rural areas since 1975, allows children to be absent in peak agricultural periods; promotes practical problem-solving rather than learning by rote; and reduces costs by allowing one teacher to cover five grades in small rural schools with the help of elected student leaders (Panel 11).

▶ *Get girls into school.* Two thirds of out-of-school children are girls, and ensuring their equal participation requires particular sensitivity to social, economic and cultural barriers. As we have seen, this is one of the most critical areas and one where

rapid improvement would produce benefits that would flow down, generation to generation.

Most initiatives aimed at drawing more children into school will also help bridge the gender gap. But specific measures are needed to overcome the social and cultural barriers for girls. High proportions of women teachers were found when UNICEF studied 10 countries where the gender gap in primary-school enrolment has narrowed.[67] Both teachers and learning materials have to be gender sensitive and avoid negative stereotypes about girls and women. Active community participation in school life, particularly by women, is essential. As experience in India indicates, when poor women become genuinely empowered to take control over their livelihoods and those of their children, remarkable changes occur.

▶ *Raise the quality and status of teachers.* Partly because of the crisis in education funding in many developing countries, the wages and status of teachers have diminished, especially at the all-important primary level. Thus, the quality of teachers entering school systems has also declined. Many have been forced to abandon teaching, or to take second and even third jobs, simply to survive. In these circumstances, many children do not see school as a place that will expand their horizons, enhance their opportunities or nurture their individual potential.

Teachers with negative and stereotypical ideas need to be retrained or replaced. Poor, low-caste or working children often are ill treated and physically abused. One response, successfully adopted by the Bangladesh Rural Advancement Committee (BRAC) in its schools, is to recruit teachers from the same community as their pupils, and to sensitize them to the children's circumstances.[68]

Of course, recruiting teachers from local communities may mean that they have less formal training. But there are creative international examples to follow. Zimbabwe, for example, achieved universal primary schooling very quickly after independence by employing untrained teachers. It therefore introduced the Zimbabwe Integrated National Teacher Education Course (ZINTEC), a four-year course in which only the first and last terms involve college attendance; the rest is spent at work in schools. ZINTEC has been successful in combining quality with low cost; training a teacher this way can be done for less than half the expense of conventional training.[69] Learning materials with detailed lesson plans for daily classroom activities ensure that teachers with modest formal training perform effectively. This approach could be valuable for many poorer countries, where many primary school teachers themselves have little more than primary education.

► *Cut the family's school bill.* Survey after survey mentions the costs of schooling as a major problem for poor families. Even when there are no tuition fees, there can be myriad other costs: for books and supplies; uniforms and shoes; transportation and lunch; not to mention the loss of the child's income.

Basic education that deters child labour must be free of such costs for poor families. But the need for financial resources goes well beyond the costs of teachers, school buildings and administration. The chronic underfunding of basic education in developing countries needs to be overcome and is a matter of global concern and responsibility, particularly because of the heavy debt burdens so many developing countries carry. For example, sub-Saharan Africa pays more than $12 billion in debt-service charges annually and owes approximately $8 billion more that it cannot pay. In comparison, just about 10 per cent of that total would provide the extra educational resources needed each year to give all the region's children a place in school.[70]

"We are trapped," said Albert Mberio, Minister of Education of the Central African Republic. "On the one hand, the Government borrows money to get our education system to work in order to obtain social and economic development. On the other hand, the same donors expect the Government to pay back borrowed money long before the country has achieved a certain level of development."[71]

The Convention on the Rights of the Child explicitly specifies in article 28 that States parties must promote and encourage international cooperation in support of developing countries' efforts to ensure access to education for all children. International organizations are moving in the right direction. The World Bank has significantly raised its lending levels for basic education in the six years since 1990. UNICEF's own medium-term target is to double its spending on basic education by the end of the decade.

There are signs, too, that bilateral aid donors are starting to place a higher priority on basic education, although within shrinking overall aid budgets. In May 1996, the Development Assistance Committee of the Organisation for Economic Co-operation and Development (OECD) committed itself to helping developing countries to reduce "absolute poverty" by half and to achieve primary education for all by the year 2015 at the latest.

Important though this external assistance is, it amounts to only about 2 per cent of the total spent by low- and middle-income countries themselves on primary education, conservatively estimated at some $270 billion annu-

The chronic underfunding of basic education in developing countries needs to be overcome and is a matter of global concern and responsibility.

ally. In other words, developing countries themselves have to mobilize the resources necessary to tackle the job that lies ahead.[72]

At the World Conference on Education for All in 1990, governments promised to increase the resources available for education. At the moment, the share of the developing world's gross national product (GNP) devoted to education expenditure averages 4 per cent, the same figure as in 1990.[73] In some of the least developed countries it is believed to have declined.

Both debt burdens and structural adjustment measures continue to make it difficult to increase education spending. Yet, except for the very poorest countries, most resources required to achieve universal primary education could be found within existing national budgets. A mid-decade review of progress in achieving education for all, held in Amman in June 1996, concluded that as many as 50 of the countries that have not enrolled all their children in school could do this quite rapidly if they made better use of their resources, by redeploying teaching staff, reallocating budgets and improving efficiency.[74] And over a third of developing countries have committed to increase spending on education.[75]

Of course, giving priority to education is not only a way of combating child labour, it is a sound economic investment. According to the World Bank, the return on investment in education in low- and middle-income countries is high — and still higher for primary schooling, compared to secondary or higher education. Primary education, says the Bank, is the largest single contributor to the economic growth rates of the high-performing Asian economies.[76] The Republic of Korea invests $130 per person per year

in basic education, and Malaysia spends $128. On the other hand, India invests just $9 per person, Pakistan $3 and Bangladesh $2.[77]

Governments must rededicate themselves to ensuring that all children receive high-quality primary education, regardless of race, gender or economic status. They can do this where necessary by adopting an incremental approach, adding a new cohort of primary school age children in phases until the target of universal primary education is reached in the shortest possible time.

In India, for example, over 100 districts are implementing a gradual approach to enrolment and retention in primary schools. Communities, district officials and teachers focus on enrolling all children aged five and six in grade 1 and increasing retention through improved quality of the classes and 'joyful learning' through grade 6. This is proving to be a practical and important strategy for preventing the entry of present and future generations into the cycle of child labour and poverty.

International agencies and development banks must give the fullest possible support to national efforts to re-establish primary education for all as an absolute priority. UNICEF, along with other international organizations, has called for governments to allocate 20 per cent of their budgets to education and basic social services, and for donor governments to do the same with their aid. Many countries have already endorsed this 20/20 initiative — it is a simple formula, easily grasped, and if the world gets behind it, it could work wonders.

Basic education can be afforded if it is made a priority, as the Convention on the Rights of the Child demands that it must be. We say again, this is a question not of scant resources but of political choice. It would cost an esti-

It would cost an estimated $6 billion a year, on top of what is already spent, to put every child in school by the year 2000. Here, a girl breaks stones for road gravel in Nepal.

UNICEF/93-1253/Noorani

mated $6 billion a year, on top of what is already spent, to put every child in school by the year 2000. That may seem an enormous sum. Yet it is less than 1 per cent of what the world spends every year on weapons.[78]

Reaching working children

Working children themselves, when given the opportunity to speak, have understandably not shown great enthusiasm for returning to an education system that has failed them in the first place. In Bamako (Mali) in 1995, for example, working children from 21 cities in 9 West African countries came together to discuss their situation. They denounced the inhuman and degrading treatment that many child workers received but also affirmed 12 basic rights to improve their lot. Among these were "the right to be taught a trade," "the right to security when working" and "the right to play... with our friends on Saturdays and Sundays." The right to go to school as their primary childhood activity was not one of their chosen 12.[79]

Studies of street children in Brazil and Paraguay have shown similar results, with most saying they would rather continue working than go back to school.[80] After experiencing dangerous freedom on the streets, these children are the least likely to respond to a formal classroom setting. This makes it all the more difficult to meet their educational needs.

Almost all attempts to bring education to working children have been through non-formal programmes, independent of the education system. One of the best known is that of BRAC, which caters to poor children aged 8 to 14 years. Although not labelled as a programme for working children, it recognizes the reality that poor children devote a major part of their day to working at home or in the fields. The BRAC school day, only two and a half hours, takes into account the daily and seasonal rhythms of life. Each small school unit of 30 children, two thirds of them girls, is located in the neighbourhood. The learning content, while based on the regular primary curriculum, emphasizes practical skills for the children's environment. The school imposes no charge of any kind on parents. The result is outstanding, with completion rates of over 95 per cent for the three-year course, after which most children enter fourth grade in the mainstream primary school.[81] By mid-1996, over 30,000 BRAC schools were offering a basic-education opportunity to close to 1 million Bangladeshi children, in urban as well as rural areas.

Another success story, which applies many of BRAC's methods, is the Barabanki project in India's Uttar Pradesh state. This caters for over 3,500 poor working children from the lowest-caste families, more than two thirds of them girls. The project takes into account the concerns of parents about trusting their girl children to the care of 'outsiders': learning centres are informal and close to home; hours are flexible; the curriculum is adapted to local conditions; and teachers come from the same caste and participate in regular in-service training. Children move from these schools into the mainstream by taking the state primary board examination.

Education can be taken to child workers even more directly. The idea of the 'street educator' has been pioneered in Latin America, though it is now being usefully imitated all over the world. In Peru, UNICEF supports a street educator project run by the National Institute for Family Well-Being. The 54 educators make contact with street children, helping them back into schools, assisting them in

Education has been part of the child labour problem and must become part of the solution. In Burundi, children in a UNICEF-assisted non-formal school share pencils, paper and ideas.

UNICEF/95-0249/Davies

Escuela Nueva: Alternative learning for rural children

UNICEF/90-0020/Tolmie

Colombia's Escuela Nueva (EN) school programme is proof that flexible, non-conventional education can get rural children into school and keep them there. More than just a methodology, Escuela Nueva is an integrated and comprehensive system of curriculum development, teacher training, administration and community mobilization. Costing only 5 to 10 per cent more than conventional schooling, it has dramatically improved the learning landscape and the lives of thousands of often forgotten students in rural areas of Colombia.

In its two decades of existence, EN has gone from local experiment to national policy, successfully introducing innovation within the government school network to serve rural children.

If conventional schooling has failed in rural areas, it is because of its inability to captivate students. Classrooms, books and supplies don't make a school — willing pupils and motivated teachers do. Too often, schooling tends to be authoritarian, inflexible, irrelevant and even hostile to children, particularly girls. Add to that the pressure children feel from families — who, especially in rural areas, may be sceptical about the value of education and open about wishing that their children were wage-earners. And the teachers often lack basic pedagogic skills. Dropping out of school to work becomes an irresistible course for many children.

To have a positive education experience, students must believe in themselves and be guided by teachers who are confident in their role. Children must feel supported by family and community and, perhaps most important, enjoy learning.

As recently as 10 years ago, half of Colombia's rural schools did not offer complete primary education. Fifty-five per cent of children between the ages of 7 and 9 and one quarter of all 10- to 14-year-olds in the countryside had never attended school. One third of all first-graders dropped out.

The dismal figures sparked a government push for universal rural primary education and rapid growth in Escuela Nueva. From 2,000 schools in 1982, the number sky-rocketed to almost 18,000 in 1989, reaching 800,000 rural children. Today, the country has over 10,000 EN schools.

Their impact has been significant. When compared with students in regular schools, EN students have scored higher on achievement tests and shown improved self-esteem, creativity and civic behaviour.

Escuela Nueva's success is the result of a number of innovations, including multigrade teaching, detailed teachers' guides and lesson plans, continuing teacher training and supervision, and involvement of the community. There is one instructor and one classroom for children at all five levels of primary education. Multigrade classes make it possible to have a complete primary school close to children's homes in sparsely populated rural areas. They also change the intimidating teacher-pupil relationship. The teacher becomes more of a facilitator, and the student a more independent learner.

Using easy-to-follow lesson guides prepared to give children an active role in learning, pupils progress on their own and with the help of older students. Learning is dynamic rather than by rote and involves play and group study, with an emphasis on practical applications and nature. Teachers, specially trained to adapt lessons to the children's surroundings, take into consideration subjects like local topography, agriculture and indigenous customs.

Promotion is flexible, not automatic: students advance from one grade to the next only when they achieve set educational objectives. This means that the school fits the timetable of the children, benefiting slower learners and children who must leave school during busy agricultural seasons. In general, pupils have more of a voice regarding their education. They monitor their own attendance and can communicate problems and concerns through suggestion boxes located at the schools.

The atmosphere also encourages learning. More than just a collection of classrooms, the schools are vibrant centres of activity that include kitchens, dining-rooms and washrooms, teacher housing, vegetable gardens, sports grounds and community facilities. Each has a small library and study corners, which are arranged by subject and display posters, minerals, artifacts, student-made crafts and other topic-related objects.

Good community relations are at the heart of the EN programme. Teachers are trained to bolster the learning process by involving parents of students and other community members in school activities. The school libraries stock supplies like agricultural calendars and monographs that contain basic information on local history, geography and culture. They double, therefore, as community information centres.

Through a strong student-government programme — in which elected student council members decide on school activities — EN schools introduce children to the ideas of democracy and foster attitudes of cooperation. And by blurring the boundary between school and community, EN relieves some of the either/or pressure children feel when faced with both school and work.

Through its innovative approach, EN has turned the traditional disadvantages of rural areas into advantages — abundant land, slower pace, bonds with nature, community contact. If keeping children in school is one of the best ways to prevent them from having to work, EN is a model system for improving the lives of rural children.

Photo: Children work together on a writing project in an Escuela Nueva programme in Colombia.

obtaining medical care and supporting attempts to reintegrate them with their families. So far, they have successfully reintegrated 1,200 children into schools.

In the Philippines, NGOs participating in the National Project on Street Children have evolved alternative education strategies for street and urban working children. Schemes ranging from 'mobile schools' to 'street schools' to 'back-to-school' programmes have reached over 60,000 street and working children across 23 cities and 9 municipalities. Local volunteers and street educators, including former street children, work alongside government officials in running the programme.

In Brazil, Projeto Axé has achieved international recognition for its imaginative educational work with the street children of Salvador. Its educators use an approach called the 'pedagogy of desire' to enable the children to make plans for the future. "The most important thing," says Axé's founder Cesare de Florio La Rocca, "is to stimulate the child to dream and wish, and to offer a number of concrete opportunities to help the child realize those dreams." Children not only learn to read and write. They can work while they study, silk-screening T-shirts or making recycled paper products, and studying in Axé's literacy programme. They can even attend Axé's circus school, where they learn to juggle, clown or fly on a trapeze. "Life on the streets is risky but also fascinating," says Mr. La Rocca. "These kids are used to risk. Here, we create positive risks and challenges." Axé has been so successful that it is now training other NGOs in its methodology of working with street children and with the municipal government to try to prevent children reaching the streets in the first place.[82]

In Brazil, Projeto Axé has achieved international recognition for its imaginative educational work with the street children of Salvador.

The choice in fact is not strictly between special non-formal programmes and the regular schools. Flexibility is the key. Education is more likely to meet the needs of working children if it reaches out to them through a range of approaches.

Local Scout groups, with UNICEF support, provide weekly literacy classes, health services and vocational training to some 150 working children in an industrial area of Alexandria (Egypt); the model project has been replicated in Cairo. And in St. Petersburg (Russian Federation), UNICEF has co-funded a non-formal education programme for street children that provides shelter, regular meals and lessons for over 200 children.

It is sometimes argued that non-formal education programmes are somehow inferior. But, as we have seen, many are successful; other non-formal approaches have not yet been fully tried and tested. And those that fail do so in part because they have lacked the necessary resources in the first place.

Bringing working children into the mainstream of the educational system is certainly the overall objective. Alternative programmes do not relieve governments of their obligations. But so far, most formal education systems have proved resistant to adapting to the circumstances of working children. The 'education for all' effort has tended to concentrate on conventional educational approaches, which bypass those children whom the system has previously failed. An inter-agency UN mission to Pakistan, for example, found that some 20 million children and young people, almost two thirds of those who will be in the age range of 10 to 18 years between 1995 and the end of the decade, have already missed primary schooling and are growing up virtually illiterate.[83]

The choice in fact is not strictly between special non-formal programmes and the regular schools. Flexibility is the key. Education is more likely to meet the needs of children if it reaches out to them through a range of formal and non-formal approaches.

Legislation

Just as the Convention on the Rights of the Child has laid down in international law new standards that national governments must strive to meet, so a country's legal code makes an important statement about what society considers to be acceptable behaviour. All countries should establish a coherent set of child labour laws both as a statement of intent and as a springboard for their wider efforts.

Another challenge confronting governments is to extend the scope of their legislation to include the informal sector, which, as this report has consistently shown, accounts for the vast majority of child labourers. More inclusive legislation would not by itself protect these children — no labour inspectorate could cover all rural areas or monitor conditions for children working in their own homes or as domestics in others'. But such legislation would provide another benchmark from which the attitudes of society could spring. It would also help establish a legal framework within which services such as community-run child care could be supplied, allowing parents to gain an income without burdening their children with the work of running home and family.

Child labour was sharply reduced in Western countries at the beginning of this century in part by combining legislation and its enforcement with compulsory primary education. Other important factors included a rise in family incomes and technological improvements that made children's labour less useful to employers. But legislation had an undeniable impact far beyond deterrence. It set new standards and changed attitudes across society. These in turn provided — and still provide — the best insurance against a return to high levels of child labour in industrialized countries.

More recently, Hong Kong has provided a notable success story, having all but eliminated child labour through:

▶ regular and persistent inspections by the Labour Department. In 1986, over 250,000 inspections were carried out in industrial and commercial establishments;
▶ special annual campaigns to detect child employment;
▶ requiring all young workers to carry identity cards with their photographs, thus facilitating enforcement;
▶ introducing welfare benefits, especially social assistance to poor families, which assured a minimum income and removed the need to rely on child labour.[84]

Of course, Hong Kong is almost completely urban and has a thriving economy. A more challenging case would be India. Legislating child labour out of existence in India, as in any other country, would be impossible in and of itself, and legislation must always be part of a comprehensive strategy. Yet laws backed by an independent, incorruptible inspectorate would be indispensable to changing attitudes to child labour right across Indian society. Such a body, with inspectors who were highly valued instead of poorly paid, undertrained and overworked, as at present, would certainly be expensive. But it should not be beyond the resources or the capabilities of India, which has recently successfully conducted and policed a general election of vast scale, overcoming enormous logistical and administrative problems and potential social turmoil.

Child labour legislation can also be a means of educating people and promoting debate on the issue. A good example of legislation being used in this educative way comes from Brazil, where children working on the street were considered a social welfare or public security problem and deemed 'delinquents', to be rounded up periodically in police sweeps. In 1982, the Government and UNICEF launched the Alternative Services for Street Children Project, building upon existing NGO and community initiatives. Child-centred policies were developed, and street children began to be seen as active and responsible agents of their own destinies.[85]

By the late 1980s, it became clear that it was not enough to rely on local initiatives. Some 500 local programmes existed, whereas 50,000 would be needed to deal with all poor urban children. The Government had to take on more active responsibility, and it did so as a result of a national debate focused on the inclusion of an article on child rights in the new Constitution. The Government established a commission to draft the article. A huge public information campaign to mobilize support for strong constitutional guarantees of children's rights ensued, resulting in a petition signed by over 1.4 million children.

The new article of the Constitution, passed by the Brazilian Congress in October 1988, read: "It is the duty of the family, of society and of the State to assure children and adolescents, with absolute priority, the right to life, health, nutrition, education, recreation, vocational preparation, culture, dignity, respect, liberty and family and community solidarity, over and beyond making them safe from neglect, discrimination, exploitation, cruelty and oppression."[86]

This was followed by the passing of the Statute on Children and

Child labour was reduced in Western countries in part by combining legislation and its enforcement with compulsory primary education. Other factors included a rise in family incomes and technological improvements that made children's labour less useful to employers.

An agreement in Bangladesh

An important initiative to protect child workers is unfolding in Bangladesh. The country's powerful garment industry is committing itself to some dramatic new measures by an agreement signed in 1995.

The country is one of the world's major garment exporters, and the industry, which employs over a million workers, most of them women, also employed child labour. In 1992, between 50,000 and 75,000 of its workforce were children under 14, mainly girls.

The children were illegally employed according to national law, but the situation captured little attention, in Bangladesh or elsewhere, until the garment factories began to hide the children from United States buyers or lay off the children, following the introduction of the Child Labor Deterrence Act in 1992 by US Senator Tom Harkin. The Bill would have prohibited the importation into the US of goods made using child labour. Then, when Senator Harkin reintroduced the Bill the following year, the impact was far more devastating: garment employers dismissed an estimated 50,000 children from their factories, approximately 75 per cent of all children in the industry.

The consequences for the dismissed children and their parents were not anticipated. The children may have been freed, but at the same time they were trapped in a harsh environment with no skills, little or no education, and precious few alternatives. Schools were either inaccessible, useless or costly. A series of follow-up visits by UNICEF, local non-governmental organizations (NGOs) and the International Labour Organization (ILO) discovered that children went looking for new sources of income, and found them in work such as stone-crushing, street hustling and prostitution — all of them more hazardous and exploitative than garment production. In several cases, the mothers of dismissed children had to leave their jobs in order to look after their children.

Out of this unhappy situation and after two years of difficult negotiations, a formal Memorandum of Understanding was signed in July 1995 by the Bangladesh Garment Manufacturers and Exporters Association (BGMEA), and the UNICEF and ILO offices in Bangladesh. The resulting programme was to be funded by these three organizations. BGMEA alone has committed about $1 million towards the implementation of the Memorandum of Understanding.

Under the terms of the agreement, four key provisions were formulated:
- the removal of all under-age workers — those below 14 — within a period of four months;
- no further hiring of under-age children;
- the placement of those children removed from the garment factories in appropriate educational programmes with a monthly stipend;
- the offer of the children's jobs to qualified adult family members.

The Memorandum of Understanding explicitly directed factory owners, in the best interests of these children, not to dismiss any child workers until a factory survey was completed and alternative arrangements could be made for the freed children.

In order to determine the extent of the educational and other rehabilitation facilities needed, a survey of all BGMEA members' factories was undertaken jointly by the three signatories in cooperation with the Government of Bangladesh. The survey of 1,821 factories found that half employed child labour, a total of 10,500 children. Forty per cent of the children were between the ages of 10 and 12, and half had no education.

With financial support from UNICEF, two NGOs — Gono Shahjjo Shangstha and the Bangladesh Rural Advancement Committee (BRAC) — have been attempting to find places in schools for these children. As of October 1996, 135 new schoolrooms were operational and more than 4,000 children were enrolled. The children are receiving primary health care, skills development training and a monthly cash stipend to compensate for their lost wages. In addition, personal bank accounts and credit facilities for their families are being set up.

The jury is still out on the long-term effectiveness of the Memorandum of Understanding. One key issue, for example, is whether setting up special schools for erstwhile child workers and providing a package of incentives such as monthly stipends, health care and skills development is a sustainable model that could be applied elsewhere and on a larger scale. Nevertheless, the events and insights that led up to the Memorandum must inform the approach of all those seeking to eliminate hazardous child labour.

The world owes child workers a meaningful alternative if they are not to suffer from some of the very measures designed to help them.

Adolescents in July 1990, which set child labour in the context of child rights by clearly stating that the welfare of the child must take precedence over all other competing interests, including those of the family. The principle established is 'children first'. Responsibility for guarding children's rights has been decentralized to the local level, specifically to watchdog councils composed equally of local government officials and NGO or community representatives.[87]

It is too early to say how successfully the new watchdog councils are protecting children from hazardous work — certainly they have not removed the necessity to enforce labour laws. And the Statute is under heavy pressure from vested interests that resent incursions on their traditional areas of influence. But it is clear that the legislation, and the process of creating it, has taken Brazilian society to a new level of debate and action.

Empowering the poor

As we have seen, poverty — and the unfair advantage that some people take of it — is a factor propelling poor children into hazardous work. Its impact can be remorseless and total, driving people to desperation, particularly when social safety nets and basic services do not exist to mitigate it. Enabling poor families to lift themselves out of the pit of powerlessness is a fundamental factor needed to bring about long-term change.

Global consensus on the need to reduce and eventually eliminate poverty was eloquently expressed in the Plan of Action emerging from the 1995 World Summit for Social Development held in Copenhagen. To reduce poverty, broad-based economic and social development is essential. The Summit called specifically for policies to create labour-intensive economic growth, to increase poor people's access to productive resources and basic services, and to ensure the adequate economic and social protection of all people.[88] Such measures would undoubtedly help reduce both the supply of and the demand for child labour.

But poor families — and especially the children within them propelled into hazardous work — need even more direct and urgent support. One key way of empowering poor families is to give them other options. We have already identified quality compulsory primary education as the most constructive alternative. But there are other ways as well.

One is to address the powerlessness that often results from class, caste or gender discrimination against a social group. In India, under the 73rd Amendment to the Constitution, community-level governing bodies are to have one third of seats reserved for women and lower-caste people, which will significantly help to correct the power balances at the village level.

Another is to provide credit to poor families in urgent need, since escape from indebtedness and from high interest rates on loans is a crucial factor in preventing bonded child labour. Successful schemes are operating in many areas of the developing world. The Grameen Bank in Bangladesh, for example, has achieved widespread international recognition for its success in providing credit to the poorest members of society — over 90 per cent of them women — who would never receive it from mainstream financial institutions. The Bank will advance only tiny sums, but tiny sums are often all that are needed to break the poverty cycle. Grameen charges current bank interest, rather than the extortionate percentages demanded by moneylenders. Today the Grameen

Poverty cannot be ended immediately, but the exploitation of poverty must no longer be tolerated. Protection from hazardous labour is a non-negotiable right for all children. A child in Egypt with his family.

61

The Grameen Bank in Bangladesh, for example, has achieved widespread international recognition for its success in providing credit to the poorest members of society — over 90 per cent of them women — who would never receive it from mainstream financial institutions.

Bank employs 14,000 staff and works in more than half of Bangladesh's 68,000 villages. It lends the equivalent of $500 million a year in nearly 4 million small-business advances to rural clients. Its social development and education programme reaches more than 12 million people. The Bank has also tried to spread its message to other parts of the developing world, and there are now 168 organizations in 44 countries aiming to replicate its achievements.[89]

The Child Labour Abolition Support Scheme (CLASS) is another example, operating in the Ambedkar District of India's Tamil Nadu state with the objective of eliminating child labour in the *beedi* (tobacco) rolling industry. Local traders, who distribute to families the leaves to be rolled into cigarettes in their homes, have also traditionally been the main source of informal credit. Children's labour is often the only security for the loan, and many young children end up in bonded servitude for years rolling cigarettes.

Begun in 1995, CLASS now operates in 49 villages, covering nearly 2,500 children and their families. Mothers' groups have been formed to promote the concept of group savings and to channel loans to members. Local banks offer subsidized loans, used to repay loans to the *beedi* traders. Primary school teachers are being retrained to be more participative and enthusiastic in their techniques, using the simple approach called 'joyful learning'. Volunteers are helping to create awareness among both the general public and government officials of the negative implications of child labour. Laws against child labour have been invoked against *beedi* traders to release children from bondage. The arrest of some traders has helped to convince others that the situation has truly changed.[90]

There is also a direct link between the extent and nature of women's participation in labour markets and child labour, making gender equity in employment another issue that must be addressed. Studies have demonstrated that the incidence of child labour declines with increases in women's incomes.

Where women do not, for a variety of reasons, hold jobs and the chances of earning incomes through other means are limited, additional pressure builds on children to work to supplement household income. Even when women do hold paying jobs, they tend to earn low wages, another factor forcing children to work. Gender equity in employment can help protect children from hazardous labour. Improving working conditions through measures such as minimum wage legislation, promotion of gender equity and the provision of child care can help to reduce the prevalence of child labour, all measures called for in the Convention on the Elimination of All Forms of Discrimination against Women.

National economic development programmes can help stimulate economic growth, raise living standards and protect families. In Mauritius, for example, the Government committed itself in the 1960s to generating employment and improving women's opportunities to work. Government investments in infrastructure created better roads and transportation and improved access to electricity, changes which, in turn, stimulated job growth and led to improved health care and education.

In Botswana, the State was similarly committed to creating jobs, multiplying work opportunities by 100 times. Between 1965 and 1980, the average annual GNP per capita growth rate grew by 10 per cent. The rise in income helped produce an increase in private spending for economic development, particularly in health care and education.[91]

Mobilizing society

The best guarantee that a government will take its responsibilities seriously is when all sectors of society become involved in a genuine national movement. As the implications of child rights and the principles of the Convention on the Rights of the Child start to permeate society, attitudes, assumptions and values will correspondingly change. And with greater community awareness comes greater involvement, leading to a powerful, if informal, labour inspectorate — of families and neighbours, strangers and friends. Such a development represents the best chance of protecting all children, but especially those farthest from official scrutiny, who are working in the informal sector and in rural areas.

▶ *NGOs* — These organizations have a vital role to play both in raising levels of public concern and protecting children. They can monitor the conditions in which children work and help launch the long, indispensable process of changing public attitudes. Their independence allows them to expose abuse or attack vested interests without yielding to political pressure. Some are deeply involved in attempts to free children from the worst dangers of work.

In India, for example, the South Asian Coalition on Child Servitude (SACCS) works with government officials in raiding sites where children are known to be working in intolerable circumstances. SACCS takes credit for either directly or indirectly being involved in the release of some 29,000 children since its inception in 1983. It bitterly points out, though,

that not a single exploiter of child labour in India has ever been imprisoned. Of the 4,000 cases registered, some 3,500 have been let off with fines of less than $6, while the rest continue to languish in the courts.[92]

NGO, church and community activism runs high in the Philippines, and for many years these groups were the only ones helping children at risk; the Marcos dictatorship routinely ignored social problems arising out of inequality and injustice. With the change in government, the situation changed, and in 1986, alarmed by the extent of child labour and child prostitution, then President Corazon Aquino declared a Year of the Protection of Filipino Exploited Children. A joint government-NGO task force began an intensive public advocacy campaign to explain the problems and launched programmes — ranging from improved-parenting workshops to schemes generating extra income for the family — to address them.[93]

One of the newest results of the continuing collaboration is the Breaking Ground project, an ambitious undertaking in 66 Filipino communities where hazardous child labour has been identified. The project enables groups of parents in the communities to meet regularly and share experiences and information on the extent of child labour. Social workers and community organizers also attend the meetings to explain child rights issues, particularly child labour concerns. The project helps parents gain skills and improve their economic opportunities so they can better protect their children, through activities to generate employment in the community and programmes for adults to improve literacy and parenting skills.

In Brazil, the National Forum for the Prevention and Elimination of

UNICEF/96-0481/Balaguer

Income-generating schemes are urgently needed to enable poor families trapped in debt to find new solutions and empower their lives. Children, such as this young boy breaking stones in Peru, have a right to develop to their full potential.

The private sector: Part of the solution

UNICEF/5863/Vilas

Insistent public pressure can be a powerful catalyst for positive social change. In response to growing public concern over the worst abuses of child labour, a number of public-minded enterprises have seized the initiative, taking steps to 'put something back' into communities where they do business. While still in a minority, these firms have demonstrated that the relationship between the private sector and activists fighting child labour need not be adversarial — that constructive co-operation, even partnership, can sometimes serve the 'best interests' of working children. Raising standards of employment and working conditions also serves to create a more efficient, stable and better-trained workforce.

The controversy over child labour in the Bangladesh garment industry illustrates just how critical a role the private sector can play — especially in an era of declining foreign aid. Negotiators seeking to phase out child labour soon realized that the industry would be a critical partner — on everything from financing

school programmes to monitoring compliance with labour standards. In the words of a UNICEF report: "The success or failure of the project hinged on their cooperation."

Another discovery was that several Bangladesh companies had already acted on their own. Among them, two garment factories — Oppex and Intersport Ltd. — opened schools on factory grounds for under-age workers and offered stipends to compensate families for the loss of children's wages.

A similar trend is emerging in Nepal's carpet industry, where child labour has been a recurring problem. Some 20 major factories have set up educational incentives, child-care and other welfare programmes. Samling Carpet Industries, for example, offers medical care, day care for their employees' youngest children and a literacy programme for school age children. Once literate, those children are sent to government schools, and their parents receive compensatory 'incentive fees' upon presentation of school reports.

Potala Carpets, one of the largest factories in the Kathmandu Valley, prefers to work through an NGO, sponsoring 30 former child weavers at a school run by the Underprivileged Children's Education Programme and the Asian-American Free Labor Institute. Another company, Formation Carpets, is an active partner with UNICEF in combating child labour in the carpet industry. The company turns over at least 1 per cent of profits, combined with employee contributions, to provide its all-adult workforce with on-site child care, scholarships for their children, health insurance, and literacy classes.

Brazil is home to vigorous campaigns against child labour, many of them fostered by the National Forum of Prevention and Eradication of Child Labour composed of goverment, non-government and multilateral organizations. For example, the Brazilian Association of Citric Exporters, which supplies 80 per cent of the international market's orange juice, pledged to eliminate child labour from its production.

Another initiative is the Abrinq Foundation, a group of nearly 2,000 businessmen and toy manufacturers formed in 1990 in the interests of child rights. Abrinq mounted a public awareness drive, using the mass media and lobbying large companies and the Government to stop buying supplies produced with child labour. One result is a recent announcement by Volkswagen, Ford, Mercedes Benz and General Motors that they will sever commercial relations with any firm that employs children. Abrinq also awards a special 'child-friendly' label to companies that prove they do not use child labour at any stage of production. In the programme's first 10 months, 150 companies earned Abrinq's stamp of approval. "We didn't expect that, in such a short time, the companies would not only agree not to use child labour, but would also actually pressure their providers to do the same," says Caio Magri, coordinator of the certification programme.

At the multinational level, the many huge corporations — most of them based in industrial countries — that use cheap child labour along the chain of production have only recently come under scrutiny. But Levi Strauss, a major garment manufacturer with production facilities in many developing countries, was looking ahead. In the 1980s, it became one of the first multinationals to address the question of social responsibility overseas, drawing up 'terms of engagement' for business partners covering environmental, ethical, health and safety standards — with a clause that bars trade with companies employing children under age 14 or below the age of compulsory schooling. In one case, Levi Strauss worked out a compromise with two Bangladesh suppliers found employing under-age workers. According to the agreement, the children were sent to school and paid wages and benefits until they were re-employed at age 14.

Other multinationals have also developed strategies to improve employment practices at the local level, in some cases asserting the right to cancel, without compensation, consignments in which child labour has been used.

Employers in the formal sector have successful models on which to base their efforts to eliminate child labour and shift from being a source of the problem to becoming part of the solution.

Photo: *A girl learns to write using a slate in a village in India.*

Child Labour, an initiative sponsored by UNICEF and ILO that involves the Government and NGOs, was established in 1994. It monitors government efforts to regulate and supervise conditions in the most grievous child labour situations, with an emphasis on children working in charcoal camps. One state-level forum has been established in Mato Grosso do Sul. And a project for children working in coal mines jointly sponsored by UNICEF and the Colombian Government has been replicated with the participation of NGOs and state agencies in other municipalities where coal is produced.

▶ *The media* — Reports on child labour carried in print and electronic media often focus on the most appalling stories of all. This is understandable and, indeed, helps to galvanize people into passionate action. The media can also be invaluable in explaining to the public the wider problems of child labour and in spreading the word about how individual initiatives have worked.

A celebrated example is that of Pagsanjan in the Philippines, which had by 1985 become a centre for child prostitution serving Western tourists. A local community organization called ROAD (Rural Organization and Assistance for Development) launched a media campaign, focusing first on Australian magazines and television stations. Over the next four years, ROAD put the issue on both the national and the international agenda. ROAD's experience is being used by the National Project on Street Children in other major cities. The Project continues to advocate media involvement in child protection issues. During the first Asian Conference on Street Children in Manila in May 1989, a national media advocacy group known as PRESSHOPE was formally launched

In countries where labour unions are weak or non-existent, collective bargaining between workers and employers can still be effective, as improvements in the working conditions of adults reduce the pressure on children to work.

under the auspices of the National Project on Street Children.[94]

The importance of mobilizing the media is now being widely recognized throughout Asia. The Asian Summit on Child Rights and the Media (Manila, July 1996) involved ministers of information, education, welfare and social development from 27 Asian countries, as well as NGO and media representatives. It declared that the media covering children's issues should address all forms of economic, commercial and sexual exploitation of children in the region — and should ensure that their own coverage does not violate child rights.

In Sri Lanka, where some hazardous child labour still persists despite a good record in school attendance, the Government launched an island-wide multimedia campaign in 1993 against the exploitation of child workers. The campaign focused particularly on child prostitution and children in domestic service. The campaign generated over 1,000 reports of abuse, compared with only 32 cases reported the year before.[95]

▶ *Trade unions* — The aims of the International Confederation of Free Trade Unions (ICFTU) are the promotion of the ILO Convention on Minimum Age for Employment and the adoption of multilateral and unilateral legal instruments to stop trade in goods produced by children.[96]

The European Trade Union Committee: Textiles, Clothing and Leather launched a campaign in 1994 to end child labour, and in 1995 the German Textile and Clothes Union followed suit. In February 1996, the Italian Committee for UNICEF, in cooperation with ILO and the Italian Ministry of Labour, launched the Labour Project, a fund- and awareness-raising campaign, with broad social support including that of trade unions and corporations. Over 15 million

workers were asked to donate one hour's wages from the extra day in the year, 29 February, to help support projects benefiting children in Bangladesh, Nepal and Pakistan. In Finland, a similar 'leap-year' campaign was launched.

In countries where labour unions are weak or non-existent, collective bargaining between workers and employers can still be effective, as improvements in the working conditions of adults reduce the pressure on children to work. Furthermore, collective bargaining can also serve the interests of working children in matters such as remuneration.

▶ *Employers* — Employers' associations are often neglected when it comes to building a broad alliance against exploitative child labour. They can be a valuable conduit for bringing influence to bear upon individual employers or sections of industry.

The Federation of Kenyan Employers, like several counterparts in other countries, implemented a programme to raise awareness among its members about the acceptable limits of child labour. It set up a plan of action to prevent and eliminate child labour among its members and to regulate working conditions, requesting members to withdraw all children from night work.[97]

UNICEF's own experience in working with the private sector has shown that corporations can be receptive to change. One initiative to which UNICEF is a major contributor is the Memorandum of Understanding concluded with employers in Bangladesh's garment industry (Panel 12).

▶ *Children* — Their role is large and growing, both in scale and influence. The story of one child, Iqbal Masih, seized the imagination and conscience of people around the world. At a very young age this Pakistani boy was given into bondage to a carpet maker. After several years of long hours and exploitative conditions, he managed one day to free himself and become part of a campaign to liberate other children. He spoke out against child labour from his own unique perspective, inspiring adults and children alike around the world.[98]

A 13-year-old Canadian, Craig Keilburger, has had a comparable impact on the North American media. When still in primary school, he set up an international organization called Free the Children, one of whose creative demands is that companies release children from work and hire an unemployed adult family member instead.

Working closely with the South Asian Coalition on Child Servitude, Craig Keilburger and Free the Children are now raising funds for a rehabilitation/education/vocational centre for freed bonded child labourers from carpet and glass factories in India's Uttar Pradesh state.[99]

Workshops and conferences in which child workers gather to exchange experiences are increasingly common. This is a welcome development, as article 15 of the Convention stipulates: "States Parties recognize the rights of the child to freedom of association." At their 1995 meeting in Bamako, working children from nine West African countries produced their own newspaper. Its editorial was written by Romaine Dieng, a domestic servant from Senegal: "The fight to obtain acceptable status in all our countries must continue. The lessons drawn from our various meetings are a reflection of [our determination]. With the daily worsening situation produced by structural adjustment and rapidly expanding poverty, self-employment [by young people] can provide a future if, and only if, it is combined with a fight for the defence of their rights by the individuals concerned."[100]

Children have the right to freedom of association, and they are exercising it. Child labourers have also formed their own organizations in the Philippines, aimed at sharing experiences, training themselves in advocacy and communicating with other child workers and the wider community through community theatre. In Olongapo City, children have formed their own separate associations for news vendors, bag sellers, scavengers, pushcart operators and bus washers. The associations also cooperate to run leadership seminars and take part in sports and recreation and in tree planting. The groups are run on democratic lines, with secret ballots at their twice-yearly meetings.

In January 1996, hundreds of children, some of them freed bonded labourers, demonstrated in front of the Indian Labour Ministry in New Delhi to demand the eradication of child servitude.[101] A month later, in a historic scene, 40 freed bonded labourers from India and Nepal, together with 25 South Asian child rights activists, marched from Calcutta to Kathmandu, holding public meetings along the route. The week-long journey ended with a large rally in Kathmandu, where they called for a mass movement aimed at the total elimination of child labour and free, compulsory, high-quality education for all children up to 14 years of age.[102]

Corporate responsibility

The accelerating impact of a liberalized international economy, led by transnational corporations, makes its own contribution to the problem of exploitative child labour.

In the global economy, many corporations locate their factories and plantations in countries with the

Workshops and conferences in which child workers gather to exchange experiences are increasingly common. This is a welcome development, as article 15 of the Convention stipulates: "States Parties recognize the rights of the child to freedom of association."

Rugmark: Helping to keep children off the looms

UNICEF/5414/Kawanaka

The Rugmark label, which pictures a smiling face on a carpet, has become the trademark for a promising new initiative to identify — and promote — products made without illegal child labour. Chartered in 1994 in India and recently extended to Nepal, the independent Rugmark Foundation provides a voluntary certification programme for carpet exporters. Rugmark awards licences — and the right to use its distinctive 'smiling carpet' logo — to carpet exporters who submit to a monitoring system that includes surprise inspections and cross-checking of export records and looms.

In addition to its monitoring and labelling activities, Rugmark is involved in children's education and rehabilitation. The first Rugmark school was opened in Bhadohi (India) in August 1996. A rehabilitation centre in Mirzapur was scheduled to open in October, modelled on the Mukti Ashram Rehabilitation project, run by the South Asian Coalition on Child Servitude (SACCS).

According to non-governmental or-

ganizations (NGOs) working in the carpet sector of Mirzapur-Bhadohi in India, the value of export earnings of the hand-knotted carpet industry in India has grown tenfold between 1979 and 1993. At the same time, they claim that the number of children working at the looms increased from 100,000 in 1975 to 300,000 in 1990. Another study, for the International Labour Organization (ILO), put the total at 420,000. Alarmed by the situation, as well as the possible threat to the carpet industry from external boycotts, a grass-roots movement of like-minded NGOs, under the direction of Kailash Satyarthi, organized in 1989 to form SACCS. In 1991, a United Nations Human Rights Commission report recommended that "products such as carpets whose manufacture is liable to involve child labour should bear a special mark guaranteeing that they have not been produced by children," giving a boost to the efforts of SACCS. Consumer groups, carpet manufacturers and international organizations joined together, with support from UNICEF and from the German Agency

for Technical Cooperation (GTZ). The result was Rugmark.

In the first 20 months of operation, Rugmark-India issued licences to more than 100 exporters operating 13,000 looms, while well over 270,000 carpets were certified, labelled and put on the market. Most of these were exported to Germany, the world's largest importer of oriental carpets, and today approximately one third of all carpets imported into Germany from India bear the Rugmark label. Meanwhile, a growing number of importers in other countries, including Canada, the Netherlands, Switzerland and the United States, are asking suppliers for Rugmark-labelled carpets.

In the first year, spot checks by independent Rugmark inspectors found 760 children working illegally on 408 looms licensed by Rugmark. As of September 1996, 164 looms were decertified; most of the others were able to pass subsequent inspections. Further, according to Satish Sondhi, Executive Director of Rugmark-India, a number of newly licensed exporters have started inspections of their own. The Indian Government has also set up an inspection and certification system for the carpet industry known as Kaleen.

Importers of Rugmark carpets agree to contribute 1 per cent of the market value of carpets imported towards schools and training programmes. The exporters also pay a fee — 0.25 per cent of the value of their carpets — which goes towards financing inspections. With these funds, it is projected that by 1998 Rugmark will pay for itself.

Rugmark operations have not been free of problems — or critics. Even strong supporters concede that surprise factory checks are not foolproof. There is a potential for corruption, along with the difficulty of inspecting 13,000 looms, in what is essentially a decentralized cottage industry. In addition, there is a pressing need to ensure that children identified by inspectors are placed in educational programmes and do not return to the looms.

To meet the challenges, Rugmark has put together a team of a dozen independent and competent inspectors, with checks and balances to minimize the possibility of corruption. In addition, each Rugmark-labelled carpet has its own number, identifying the loom and exporter. The Rugmark labels are prepared individually, corresponding to the purchase order of the carpet. The network of controls is, therefore, highly organized and advocates say that so far not one falsely labelled carpet has been identified by critics.

When Rugmark-Nepal begins its operation, it will be two-pronged, focusing on inspecting looms, as well as on ensuring that children released from the looms are placed immediately in schools and not left to fend for themselves in risky situations. As of September 1996, 30 large manufacturers, representing 70 per cent of Nepal's carpet exports, have committed to obtaining Rugmark licences.

Christian Salazar-Volkmann of the German Committee for UNICEF believes Rugmark's initiative is one way of reviving consumer interest. "What has happened is a turnaround," he says. "Now they are seeing Rugmark as a marketing opportunity."

Photo: Rugmark Foundation is soon to begin operations in Nepal. These two girls work on a loom at a Kathmandu carpet factory.

cheapest labour or the weakest trade unions. Some avoid even owning factories or plantations, subcontracting production to local enterprises or workshops.

All workers, communities and countries have effectively become competitors for the favours of transnational corporations. Efforts by national governments or workers to improve pay and conditions, or to restrict a foreign corporation's activities, may prompt the corporation to simply move elsewhere.

An example from South Africa illustrates the point. Encouraged by the election of Nelson Mandela's Government, the black women who worked in a Taiwanese-owned sweater factory asked for improved wages and the right to join a union. The company's response was to close down all seven of its South African factories, putting 1,000 people out of work. The wages they had to pay in South Africa may have been low, but they were higher than those in China or Thailand.[103]

The worldwide drive for competitiveness draws children into the workforce. In India, which has only in recent years opened up fully to the global economy, international competition has already led some sectors of industry to seek an advantage by recruiting cheap child labour — children's wages in Indian industry are less than half those of adults for the same output. Increases in child labour are reported in sericulture, fish processing, food processing and the genetic engineering of seeds.[104]

Corporate behaviour is best influenced at the international level. A fierce debate currently rages over whether a social clause should be included in the rules of the World Trade Organization and in regional trading agreements. Such a clause would lay down minimum standards

All workers, communities and countries have effectively become competitors for the favours of transnational corporations.

It is time morality prevailed. As we step into the next millennium, hazardous child labour must be left behind, consigned to history as completely as those other forms of slavery that it so closely resembles.

of corporate behaviour as a condition of doing business globally. And it would include prohibitions on using child labour.

Developing countries, especially those in Asia and Latin America, have dismissed the social clause as disguised protectionism. Their main argument has been that wage levels and social protection depend on each country's level of development and that a social clause would stifle the development of low-wage countries by depriving them of their main comparative advantage in international trade. Many employers in industrialized countries — together with some European governments — also reject the social clause. France and the US are strongly in favour.

Religious, consumer, environmental and human rights groups are taking more direct measures to influence transnationals, pressuring them to adopt, for themselves and their subcontractors, codes of conduct for operations in poorer countries.

The Interfaith Center on Corporate Responsibility (ICCR), for example, has been campaigning for 25 years in favour of corporate accountability. In recent years, ICCR members filed shareholder resolutions with a range of companies, including well-known clothing and shoe manufacturers, calling on them to adopt or amend codes of conduct for themselves and their suppliers. Several provisions are essential for effective company codes, according to ICCR. They should specifically prohibit child labour and contain provisions on freedom of association, sustainable wage and compliance and monitoring.

Some corporations have already adopted codes, guaranteeing that neither they nor their subcontractors will employ children in conditions that violate national laws or that adversely affect children's rights, development

or education (Panel 13). In 1992, for example, Levi Strauss found that two of its Bangladeshi contractors employed children under the age of 14. This was legal in Bangladesh but contravened the company's own guidelines. They arranged for the children concerned to be paid while they attended school, and promised them jobs when they turned 14.[105] Another example is the code adopted by the British retailer C&A, which states: "Exploitation of child labour or the exploitation of any other vulnerable group — for example, illegal immigrants — is absolutely unacceptable."[106]

In another case, the retail clothing giant Gap came under considerable public pressure in the US when the fact emerged that girls as young as 13 were making garments for the company, working up to 70 hours a week in dismal El Salvador sweatshops, and being paid less than $0.60 an hour. Gap agreed to insist that its local contractors respect basic workers' rights and to allow independent monitoring of its own code of conduct.[107] The Independent Monitoring Working Group, formed in January 1996 by ICCR, Business for Social Responsibility and the US-based National Labor Committee, is responsible for coordinating the monitoring of Gap suppliers and recruited four respected religious, labour and human rights groups in El Salvador to conduct factory checks.[108]

Successes like these have led to closer scrutiny of clothing, footwear and toy corporations that have shifted a great deal of their production overseas. The challenge now is to extend this notion of corporate responsibility for child labour — and the campaigning that can bring it about — to national companies. The Abrinq Foundation for the Rights of Children in Brazil is one organization — financed by the private sector — that is already hard at work on this. Abrinq has received considerable media attention for its accusation that giant international automobile makers used charcoal produced by a particularly hazardous form of child labour. But the Foundation also keeps watch on domestic companies, and its child-friendly company programme calls positive attention to Brazilian businesses that do not employ children and that support child-development activities (Panel 13).[109]

All companies — even those that do not hire or exploit children — can be harmed by the negative publicity and global criticism associated with hazardous child labour practices. Clearly, it is in the interests of all companies to lend their weight to the movement to abolish child labour.

A break with the past

Growing children are eager to learn about the world — about its mechanics and its wonders, its customs and its rules. They soak up information with miraculous ease, as if knowledge itself were fuelling their development, learning from the world around them, from school, from play, from parents, from teachers, from other children and sometimes also from work.

What kind of learning, however, is a child to derive from work in domestic service, labouring in isolation from family and community? What new mental horizons are opened by the working experience of a child sold into bonded labour? What terrifying lessons is a child prostitute required to learn every day? These most unrelenting, punishing forms of child labour violate most of the rights in the Convention on the Rights of the Child and the basic humanity of all of us.

The same grotesque skewing of priorities that leaves so many children without adequate nutrition, immunization and health care also leads to children being exploited and damaged by work. Those priorities must now change: the world's governments have recognized children's absolute right to unfettered physical, social and emotional development and must be held to their word. As this report has repeatedly stated, basic primary education for all children is a keystone of these rights, and in some ways a condition for the exercise of other rights.

Child labour is so emotive an issue precisely because it brings people face to face with the human consequences of a world that is becoming ever more unequal. The emotion it provokes must fuel a charge against the unrelenting oppression and maltreatment of girls, the denial of education to 140 million of the world's children, and the economic system that demands that the poorest must tighten their belts to pay off debts incurred by a previous generation.

It is time morality prevailed. As we step into the next millennium, hazardous child labour must be left behind, consigned to history as completely as those other forms of slavery that it so closely resembles.

The most important action is prevention: ensuring that today's children, like this Vietnamese boy, and future generations of children are not driven into hazardous labour.

UNICEF/93-1304/Frieger

Ending child labour:
The next steps

Hazardous and exploitative child labour violates child rights as enshrined in the Convention on the Rights of the Child. Immediate action to eliminate such labour must be guided by the best interests of the child. Concern for the well-being of families whose survival may depend upon the earnings of their children must include efforts to expand job opportunities for adults.

Since the causes of child labour are complex and include poverty, economic exploitation, social values and cultural circumstances, solutions must be comprehensive and must involve the widest possible range of partners in each society.

Some specific actions that are urgently needed are as follows:

1. Immediate elimination of hazardous and exploitative child labour

Hazardous and exploitative forms of child labour, including bonded labour, commercial sexual exploitation and work that hampers the child's physical, social, cognitive, emotional or moral development, must not be tolerated, and governments must take immediate steps to end them.

2. Provision of free and compulsory education

Governments must fulfil their responsibility to make relevant primary education free and compulsory for all children (article 28 of the Convention) and ensure that all children attend primary school on a full-time basis until completion. Governments must budget the necessary resources for this purpose, with donors ensuring adequate resources from existing development aid budgets.

3. Wider legal protection

Laws on child labour and education should be consistent in purpose and implemented in a mutually supportive way. National child labour laws must accord with both the spirit and letter of the Convention and with relevant ILO conventions. Such legislation must encompass the vast majority of child work in the informal sector of the economy, including work on the streets and farms, domestic work or work within the child's own household.

4. Birth registration of all children

All children should be registered at birth (article 7 of the Convention). Registration is essential to permit the exercise of the child's rights, such as access to education, health care and other services, as well as to provide employers and labour inspectors with evidence of every child's age.

5. Data collection and monitoring

Data on child labour are scarce. National and international systems must be put in place to gather and analyse globally comparable data on child labour, if the problem is to be addressed effectively. Special attention must be paid to the forgotten or 'invisible' areas of child labour, such as within the home, on the family farm or in domestic service. Monitoring by communities themselves is important, and working children should actively participate in assessing their situations and in proposing ways to improve their conditions.

6. Codes of conduct and procurement policies

National and international corporations are urged to adopt codes of conduct guaranteeing that neither they nor their subcontractors will employ children in conditions that violate their rights. Procurement policies must be developed to take into account the best interests of the child and include measures to protect those interests. UNICEF reaffirms its commitment to its own procurement policy, through which it undertakes not to buy from any supplier that exploits children.

References

Chapter I: The Convention on the Rights of the Child

1 UNICEF, *The Progress of Nations 1996,* UNICEF, New York, 1996, pp. 38-40.

2 UNICEF, *The State of the World's Children 1996,* UNICEF, New York, 1995, p. 10; and UNICEF, *The Progress of Nations 1996,* p. 23.

3 UNDP, *Human Development Report 1996,* UNDP, New York, 1996, p. 12.

4 UNICEF, *The 20/20 Initiative: Achieving universal access to basic social services for sustainable human development, A note prepared jointly by UNDP, UNESCO, UNFPA, UNICEF and WHO,* UNICEF, New York, 1994, p. 5.

5 UNDP, *Human Development Report 1994,* UNDP, New York, 1994, p. 50.

Chapter II: Children at risk: Ending hazardous and exploitative child labour

1 Lee-Wright, Peter, *Child Slaves,* Earthscan, London, 1990, p. 40.

2 'Child Labour in Britain', report to the International Working Group on Child Labour, September 1995, p. 34.

3 ILO, *World Labour Report 1992,* ILO, Geneva, 1992, p. 14.

4 Pollack, S. H., et al., 'The Health Hazards of Agricultural Child Labor', in *Migrant Health: Clinical supplement,* May-June 1990, cited in A. Bequele and W. E. Myers, *First Things First in Child Labour: Eliminating work detrimental to children,* UNICEF/ILO, Geneva, 1995, p. 4.

5 Draft Declaration, Meeting of Ministers of Labour of the Non-Aligned Movement and Other Developing Countries, New Delhi, 23 January 1996.

6 US Bureau of International Labor Affairs, *By the Sweat and Toil of Children: The use of child labor in US manufactured and mined imports,* Vol. 1, US Department of Labor, Washington, D.C., 1994, p. 2.

7 Carriere, Rolf, 'In the Child's Best Interest: Planning for and progressively eliminating child labour', unpublished presentation, Feb. 1996, p. 3.

8 Heissler, Karin, 'Child Labour in Export Garment Manufacturing: Towards an understanding of the industry, implications for development and interventions for children', unpublished manuscript, 19 Dec. 1995, p. 64.

9 UNICEF, 'Exploitation of working children and street children', Executive Board document E/ICEF/1986/CRP.3, 14 March 1986, pp. 3-4.

10 Bequele, A., and W. E. Myers, *First things first in child labour: Eliminating work detrimental to children,* UNICEF/ILO, Geneva, 1995, pp. 6-7.

11 Statement by Dr. Mark Belsey, WHO, cited in Annie Allsebrook and Anthony Swift, *Broken Promise,* Hodder and Stoughton, London, 1989, p. 91.

12 Bequele and Myers, op. cit., pp. 13-14.

13 Bequele, Assefa, and Jo Boyden, *Combating Child Labour,* ILO, Geneva, 1988, p. 10.

14 Ibid.

15 ILO Minimum Age Convention, 1973 (No. 138).

16 ILO, press materials issued with 'Child Labour: What is to be done?', document for discussion at the Informal Tripartite Meeting at the Ministerial Level, Geneva, 12 June 1996.

17 ILO/IPEC, press release for *Child Labour Surveys: Results of methodological experiments in four countries 1992-93,* ILO, Geneva, 4 April 1996.

18 Report of the ILO Governing Body, 265th Session, Geneva, March 1996, p. 4.

19 ILO, *World Labour Report 1992,* p. 13.

20 United Nations Economic Commission for Latin America and the Caribbean, *Social Panorama of Latin America,* ECLAC, Santiago (Chile), 1995, pp. 54-55.

21 Ibid., p. 38.

22 Burra, Neera, *Born to Work: Child labour in India,* Oxford University Press, Delhi, 1995, pp. 228-229.

23 Zimbabwe Government report, cited in ILO, *Towards Action Against Child Labour in Zimbabwe,* ILO, Geneva, 1992, p. 53.

24 UNDP, *Human Development Report 1996,* UNDP, p. 72.

25 Ahmed, Manzoor, and Mary Joy Pigozzi, 'The power of education', unpublished manuscript, 15 July 1996, p. 4.

26 World Bank, *Priorities and Strategies for Education: A World Bank review,* World Bank, Washington, D.C., 1995, p. 41.

27 Instituto Nacional de Educação e Pesquisa, Brasília, 1994.

28 Weiner, Myron, *The Child and the State in India,* Princeton University Press, Princeton, 1991, pp. 5-6.

29 Minnesota Lawyers International Human Rights Committee, 'Restavek: Child labour in Haiti', case report, Minneapolis, 1990, quoted by Bill Salter in an unpublished research paper for ILO on domestic service, pp. 30, 35, 46.

30 Salter, op. cit., pp. 12-14.

31 Ibid., p. 23.

32 Chaney, Elsa M., and Mary Garcia Castro (eds.), *Muchachas No More: Household workers in Latin America and the Caribbean,* Temple University Press, Philadelphia, 1989, cited in Salter, op. cit., p. 43.

33 Salter, op. cit., p. 44.

34 Comlan, Elvire, 'Le Travail des enfants en République populaire du Bénin; le cas des filles vidomégon de Cotonou', unpublished thesis, National University of Benin, 1987, quoted in Salter, op. cit., p. 52.

35 Salter, op. cit., p. 54.

36 Ibid., p. 53.

37 Black, Maggie, 'Research methods relating to child domestic workers', summary report of the Anti-Slavery International Seminar held at Charney Manor, Oxfordshire (UK), 22-24 January 1996.

38 Salter, op. cit., pp. 80-81.

39 Burra, op. cit., p. 21.

40 Sutton, Alison, *Slavery in Brazil: A link in the chain of modernisation,* Anti-Slavery International, London, 1994, p. 70.

41 Ibid., p. 29.

42 Jacobs, Charles, and Mohamed Athie, 'Bought and Sold', *The New York Times,* 13 July 1994.

43 Gupta, M., 'Child Labour in Hazardous Work in India: Situation and policy experience', unpublished study for ILO, 1989, quoted in Bequele and Myers, op. cit., p. 8.

44 Weiner, Myron, Foreword, in Burra, op. cit., pp. x-xi.

45 ILO, *Towards Action Against Child Labour in Zimbabwe*, pp. 46-47.

46 'Child Workers in the Tobacco Industry, Indonesia', in *Child Workers in Asia*, Vol. 7, No. 1, Jan.-Mar. 1991, p. 15.

47 'Child Workers in the Tea Industry in Nepal', in *Child Workers in Asia*, pp. 3-4.

48 'Child Labour in the Agricultural Sector in Thailand: A case study of child workers in the sugar cane and the rubber plantation', in *Child Workers in Asia*, p. 10.

49 Testimony presented by a Honduran worker to a US Congressional committee, as cited in Bob Herbert, 'Leslie Fay's Logic', *The New York Times*, 19 June 1994.

50 Serrill, Michael S., 'Unholy Confession: A cop on trial for a massacre of street children stuns Brazil by admitting an appalling crime', *Time*, 13 May 1996, p. 33.

51 Rosario, A., 'Ragpicking and ragpickers' education and development scheme in Bangalore City', in *Prevention and protection of working children and abandoned children*, country reports and case studies, Second Asian Regional Conference on Child Abuse and Neglect, Bangkok, 8-13 February 1988, cited in Bequele and Myers, op. cit., p. 3.

52 Swift, Anthony, 'Scared of our own kids', *The New Internationalist*, No. 276, February 1996, pp. 14-16.

53 Johnson, Victoria, Joanna Hill and Edda Ivan-Smith, *Listening to Smaller Voices: Children in an environment of change*, ActionAid, London, 1995, p. 77.

54 Salazar, Maria Cristina, and Walter Alarcón Glasinovich, *Better Schools, Less Child Work: Child work and education in Brazil, Colombia, Ecuador, Guatemala and Peru*, Innocenti Essays VII, UNICEF International Child Development Centre, Florence, 1996.

55 Burra, op. cit., 211.

56 Salazar and Alarcón Glasinovich, op. cit., p. 19.

57 UNICEF, *The Progress of Nations 1996*, p. 30.

58 UNICEF, *The State of the World's Children 1996*, p. 86.

59 Boyden, Jo, *The Relationship between Education and Child Work*, Innocenti Occasional Papers, Child Rights Series No. 9, UNICEF International Child Development Centre, Florence, 1994, p. 21.

60 'World Declaration on the Survival, Protection and Development of Children', para. 15, as cited in UNICEF, *The State of the World's Children 1991*, UNICEF, New York, 1990, p. 54.

61 Ibid., para. 19, p. 55.

62 Ibid., para. 20, item 7, p. 56.

63 'Plan of Action for implementing the World Declaration on the Survival, Protection and Development of Children in the 1990s', para. 23, as cited in UNICEF, *The State of the World's Children 1991*, op. cit., 1990, p. 66.

64 UNICEF data and UNESCO, *Trends and Projections of Enrolment by Level of Education, by Age and by Sex, 1960-2025 (as assessed in 1993)*, UNESCO, Paris, 1993.

65 ILO, 'Child Labour: What is to be done?', p. 23.

66 Concerned for Working Children, 'Education: Views of the working children', report based on discussions held during the Appropriate Education Workshop held in Namma Bhooomi, Gramashrama (India), April 1995.

67 Mehrotra, Santosh, 'Health and Education Policies in the High-Achieving Countries: Some lessons', in Santosh Mehrotra and Richard Jolly (eds.), *Development with a Human Face*, draft, to be published by Oxford University Press, p. 43.

68 Ahmed, Manzoor, et al., *Primary Education for All: Learning from the BRAC experience*, Academy for Educational Development, Washington, D.C., 1993, p. 41.

69 Mehrotra, op. cit., pp. 37-38.

70 World Bank, *World Debt Tables 1996: External finance for developing countries*, Vol. 1, Analysis and Summary Tables, World Bank, Washington, D.C., 1996, p. 216.

71 'Funding: Counting the Cost of Education for All', in *Education for All: Achieving the Goal*, press kit for the Mid-Decade Meeting of the International Consultative Forum on Education for All, Amman, 16-19 June 1996, UNESCO, Paris, May 1996.

72 World Bank, *Priorities and Strategies for Education: A World Bank Review*, op. cit., p. 153.

73 UNESCO, *World Education Report 1995*, UNESCO, Paris, 1995, p. 109.

74 Jolly, Richard, concluding statement at the Mid-decade Meeting of the International Consultative Forum on Education for All, Amman, 16-19 June 1996, pp. 5-6.

75 *Education for All: Achieving the Goal*, statistical document for the Mid-Decade Meeting of the International Consultative Forum on Education for All, Amman, 16-19 June 1996, pp. 30-33.

76 World Bank, *Priorities and Strategies for Education: A World Bank Review*, op. cit., p. 23.

77 Haq, Mahbub ul, 'If people sleep on pavements, should ministers shop for modern jets?', *The Times of India*, New Delhi, 28 March 1996, p. 11.

78 UNICEF, *The 20/20 Initiative: Achieving universal access to basic social services for sustainable human development*; and UNDP, *Human Development Report 1994*, p. 48.

79 *A Letter from the Street*, liaison and support bulletin for working children and shanty town children produced by ENDA-Tiers Monde (Dakar), No. 14, February 1996, p. 4.

80 Bequele and Myers, op. cit., p.138.

81 Ahmed, Manzoor, et al., op cit., pp. xii-xiii, 75.

82 Lewnes, Alexia, 'Learning to dream at Projeto Axé', *First Call for Children*, April/June 1994, p. 3.

83 UNICEF, 'Challenges and Opportunities: Basic education for all in Pakistan', report of a UN Inter-agency Mission on Basic Education, 1995, as cited in Ahmed and Pigozzi, op. cit., p. 9.

84 Bequele and Boyden, op. cit., pp. 179-181.

85 Boyden, Jo, and William Myers, *Exploring Alternative Approaches to Combating Child Labour: Case studies from developing countries*, Innocenti Occasional Papers, Child Rights Series No. 8, UNICEF International Child Development Centre, Florence, 1995, p. 20.

86 Ibid., pp. 22-23.

87 Ibid., pp. 23-24.

88 Report of the World Summit for Social Development, Copenhagen, 6-12 March 1995 (A/CONF.166/9, 19 April 1995).

89 Ali, Shan, 'Eliminating poverty', *The New Internationalist*, No. 274, December 1995, p. 5.

90 *Elimination of Child Labour in North Arcot, Ambedkar District in Tamil Nadu,* undated manuscript from UNICEF, New Delhi.

91 UNICEF, *Profiles in Success: People's progress in Africa, Asia and Latin America*, UNICEF, New York, 1995, pp. 12, 15-16.

92 'Meeting on child labour held', *The Statesman* (Calcutta), 1 March 1996, p. 3; and interview with Kailash Satyarthi, Chair of SACCS, 30 March 1996.

93 Boyden and Myers, op. cit., p. 15.

94 Rialp, Victoria, *Children and Hazardous Work in the Philippines*, ILO, Geneva, 1993, pp. 28-34.

95 Statement for the International Textile, Garment and Leather Workers' Federation; Textile Workers Asian Regional Organization and Friedrich Ebert Stiftung Foundation, Regional Workshop on Child Labour in South Asia, Kathmandu, 26-30 Sept. 1994, p. 11.

96 'Workers campaign', *Children and Work*, ILO/IPEC, June 1995, p. 5.

97 ILO/IPEC, *Implementation Report: Review of IPEC experience 1992-95,* ILO/IPEC, Geneva, Oct. 1995, pp. 29-30.

98 Interview with Muhammad Mushtaq of Insan Foundation, Lahore, 22 March 1996.

99 Canadian International Development Agency, 'Canada supports program to end child labour', news release, 13 Feb. 1996; Jeff Sallot, 'Canada targets overseas child sex', *Globe and Mail,* 4 April 1996; Rosemary Speirs, 'Trading carefully on a child labour policy', *Toronto Star,* 15 Feb. 1996; Carol Goar, 'Teenager's child labour plea hailed in US', *Toronto Star,* 30 April 1996, p. A14.

100 *A Letter from the Street*, p. 1.

101 'Hundreds of freed bonded children demonstrate', *The Asian Age,* 2 Jan.1996; Chakrabarti, Ashis, 'Freed child labourers plan march to Nepal', *Indian Express,* 1 March 1996.

102 'Plea to put an end to child labour', *The Rising Nepal* (Kathmandu), 7 March 1996; 'A march to break the shackles', *The Pioneer (*New Delhi), 15 March 1996.

103 Korten, David C., *When Corporations Rule the World*, Kumarian Press/Berrett-Koehler, West Hartford/San Francisco, 1995, pp. 230-231.

104 Burra, op. cit., p. 253.

105 Nichols, Martha, 'Third World Families at Work: Child labor or child care?' *Harvard Business Review,* Jan.-Feb. 1993, p. 16.

106 'The Business of Child Labour', *Anti-Slavery Reporter*, July 1996.

107 Cavanagh, John, and Robin Broad, 'Global Reach: Workers fight the multinationals', *The Nation*, 18 March 1996, p. 22.

108 Schilling, David M., testimony at the International Child Labor Public Hearing, US Department of Labor, Washington, DC, 28 June 1996.

109 'Quen lucra como trabalho infantil', in *Atenção*, published by the Abrinq Foundation for the Rights of Children, São Paulo, Dec. 1995/Jan. 1996; and open letters from Abrinq to all government departments, to the Chair of the Brazilian Association of Exporters of Citrus Fruits and to the Chair of the National Association of Manufacturers of Automotive Vehicles, 23 Jan. 1996.

Chapter III

Statistical tables

Economic and social statistics on the nations of the world, with particular reference to children's well-being.

General note on the data

The data provided in these tables are accompanied by definitions, sources, and explanations of symbols. Tables derived from so many sources - 13 major sources are listed in the explanatory material — will inevitably cover a wide range of data quality. Official government data received by the responsible United Nations agency have been used whenever possible. In the many cases where there are no reliable official figures, estimates made by the responsible United Nations agency have been used. Where such internationally standardized estimates do not exist, the tables draw on other sources, particularly data received from the appropriate UNICEF field office. Where possible, only comprehensive or representative national data have been used.

Data quality is likely to be adversely affected for countries that have recently suffered from man-made or natural disasters. This is particularly so where basic country infrastructure has been fragmented or major population movements have occurred.

Data for life expectancy, crude birth and death rates, infant mortality rates, etc. are part of the regular work on estimates and projections undertaken by the United Nations Population Division. These and other internationally produced estimates are revised periodically, which explains why some of the data will differ from those found in earlier UNICEF publications.

The statistical tables in the present report include a substantial amount of new data, particularly for ORT use and maternal mortality. In addition, a new indicator, the percentage of households consuming iodized salt, has been included in table 2.

The ORT data reflect UNICEF and WHO support for the development of timely, reliable national estimates. While there are still many data gaps, ORT figures are reported for countries covering almost 90% of the world's under-five population.

The maternal mortality data represent a major first step in deriving more consistent estimates. Data used in past reports lacked consistency, both in adjustments to national data for biases, and for country estimates where no national coverage data were available. The present estimates result from a dual approach by UNICEF and WHO, where national data are adjusted for misclassification and underreporting, and a consistent approach used to predict values for countries lacking reliable national data.

Explanation of symbols

Since the aim of this statistics chapter is to provide a broad picture of the situation of children and women worldwide, detailed data qualifications and footnotes are seen as more appropriate for inclusion elsewhere. Only two symbols are used in the tables.

..   Data not available.

x   Indicates data that refer to years or periods other than those specified in the column heading, differ from the standard definition, or refer to only part of a country.

Note: Child mortality estimates for individual countries are primarily derived from data reported by the United Nations Population Division. In some cases, these estimates may differ from the latest national figures. In general, data released during approximately the last year are not incorporated in these estimates.

Index to countries

In the following tables, countries are ranked in descending order of their estimated 1995 under-five mortality rate. The reference numbers indicating that rank are given in the alphabetical list of countries below.

Afghanistan	5	Ghana	35	Peru	65
Albania	76	Greece	128	Philippines	67
Algeria	62	Guatemala	58	Poland	114
Angola	2	Guinea	7	Portugal	123
Argentina	95	Guinea-Bissau	6	Romania	94
Armenia	90	Haiti	37	Russian Federation	93
Australia	135	Honduras	81	Rwanda	32
Austria	140	Hong Kong*	147	Saudi Arabia	87
Azerbaijan	70	Hungary	119	Senegal	43
Bangladesh	38	India	39	Sierra Leone	3
Belarus	106	Indonesia	53	Singapore	148
Belgium	127	Iran, Islamic Rep. of	79	Slovakia	116
Benin	31	Iraq	57	Slovenia	134
Bhutan	17	Ireland	143	Somalia	10
Bolivia	47	Israel	132	South Africa	59
Bosnia and Herzegovina	113	Italy	136	Spain	129
Botswana	68	Jamaica	121	Sri Lanka	110
Brazil	63	Japan	146	Sudan	40
Bulgaria	108	Jordan	98	Sweden	150
Burkina Faso	23	Kazakstan	73	Switzerland	142
Burundi	20	Kenya	49	Syrian Arab Rep.	84
Cambodia	21	Korea, Dem. Peo. Rep.	92	Tajikistan	51
Cameroon	46	Korea, Rep. of	130	Tanzania , U. Rep. of	25
Canada	139	Kuwait	120	TFYR Macedonia	91
Central African Rep.	22	Kyrgyzstan	66	Thailand	89
Chad	27	Lao Peo. Dem. Rep.	34	Togo	36
Chile	117	Latvia	97	Trinidad and Tobago	112
China	72	Lebanon	80	Tunisia	82
Colombia	83	Lesotho	26	Turkey	71
Congo	45	Liberia	9	Turkmenistan	50
Costa Rica	115	Libyan Arab Jamahiriya	60	Uganda	18
Côte d'Ivoire	28	Lithuania	109	Ukraine	100
Croatia	118	Madagascar	24	United Arab Emirates	111
Cuba	124	Malawi	8	United Kingdom	141
Czech Rep.	126	Malaysia	122	United States	125
Denmark	145	Mali	11	Uruguay	105
Dominican Rep.	75	Mauritania	15	Uzbekistan	61
Ecuador	77	Mauritius	103	Venezuela	101
Egypt	69	Mexico	88	Viet Nam	74
El Salvador	78	Moldova	85	Yemen	44
Eritrea	13	Mongolia	55	Yugoslavia	102
Estonia	104	Morocco	54	Zaire	19
Ethiopia	14	Mozambique	4	Zambia	12
Finland	149	Myanmar	29	Zimbabwe	56
France	131	Namibia	52		
Gabon	30	Nepal	41		
Gambia	42	Netherlands	137		
Georgia	96	New Zealand	133		
Germany	144	Nicaragua	64		
		Niger	1		
		Nigeria	16		
		Norway	138		
		Oman	99		
		Pakistan	33		
		Panama	107		
		Papua New Guinea	48		
		Paraguay	86	*Colony	

Table 1: Basic indicators

		Under-5 mortality rate		Infant mortality rate (under 1)		Total population (millions) 1995	Annual no. of births (thousands) 1995	Annual no. of under-5 deaths (thousands) 1995	GNP per capita (US$) 1994	Life expectancy at birth (years) 1995	Total adult literacy rate 1995	Primary school enrolment ratio (gross) 1990-95	% share of household income 1990-94	
		1960	1995	1960	1995								lowest 40%	highest 20%
1	Niger	320	**320**	191	191	9.2	472	151	230	48	14	29	19	44
2	Angola	345	**292**	208	170	11.1	555	162	700x	48	42x	88	..	..
3	Sierra Leone	385	**284**	219	164	4.5	216	61	160	40	31	51	..	..
4	Mozambique	331	**275**	190	158	16.0	711	196	90	47	40	60	..	..
5	Afghanistan	360	**257**	215	165	20.1	1041	268	280x	45	32	31	..	..
6	Guinea-Bissau	336	**227**	200	134	1.1	45	10	240	45	55	60x	9	59
7	Guinea	337	**219**	203	128	6.7	331	73	520	46	36	46	11	50
8	Malawi	365	**219**	206	138	11.1	540	118	170	45	56	80	..	..
9	Liberia	288	**216**	192	144	3.0	140	30	450x	56	38	35x	..	..
10	Somalia	294	**211**	175	125	9.3	461	97	120x	48	24x	11x	..	..
11	Mali	400	**210**	233	117	10.8	532	112	250	47	31	31	..	..
12	Zambia	220	**203**	135	114	9.5	409	83	350	48	78	92	12	50
13	Eritrea	294	**195**	175	114	3.5	147	29	100x	52	..	47	..	..
14	Ethiopia	294	**195**	175	114	55.1	2597	506	100	49	36	23	21	41
15	Mauritania	321	**195**	191	112	2.3	89	17	480	53	38	69	14x	47x
16	Nigeria	204	**191**	122	114	111.7	4915	939	280	51	57	93	13	49
17	Bhutan	324	**189**	203	122	1.6	64	12	400	52	42	25x	..	..
18	Uganda	218	**185**	129	111	21.3	1071	198	190	44	62	67	17	48
19	Zaire	286	**185**	167	119	43.9	2035	377	220x	52	77	68	..	..
20	Burundi	255	**176**	151	106	6.4	283	50	160	51	35	69	..	..
21	Cambodia	217	**174**	146	110	10.3	414	72	200x	53	35x	..	..	..
22	Central African Rep.	294	**165**	174	106	3.3	135	22	370	50	60	71x	..	..
23	Burkina Faso	318	**164**	183	86	10.3	471	77	300	47	19	38	..	..
24	Madagascar	364	**164**	219	100	14.8	628	103	200	58	80x	73	16	50
25	Tanzania, U.Rep.of	249	**160**	147	100	29.7	1252	200	140	52	68	70	18	45
26	Lesotho	204	**154**	138	105	2.1	74	11	720	62	71	98	9x	60x
27	Chad	325	**152**	195	94	6.4	273	42	180	49	48	59	..	..
28	Côte d'Ivoire	300	**150**	195	90	14.3	697	105	610	50	40	69	18x	44x
29	Myanmar	237	**150**	158	105	46.5	1468	220	220x	59	83	105	..	..
30	Gabon	287	**148**	171	89	1.3	51	8	3880	55	63	..	..	..
31	Benin	310	**142**	184	85	5.4	257	37	370	48	37	66	..	..
32	Rwanda	191	**139**	115	80	8.0	346	48	80	47	61	77	23x	39x
33	Pakistan	221	**137**	137	95	140.5	5513	755	430	63	38	44	21	40
34	Lao Peo. Dem. Rep.	233	**134**	155	91	4.9	211	28	320	52	57	107	23	40
35	Ghana	213	**130**	126	76	17.5	708	92	410	57	65	76	20	42
36	Togo	264	**128**	155	80	4.1	180	23	320	56	52	102	..	..
37	Haiti	260	**124**	170	71	7.2	250	31	230	58	45	56	..	..
38	Bangladesh	247	**115**	151	85	120.4	4149	477	220	57	38	79	23	38
39	India	230	**115**	144	76	935.7	26106	3002	320	62	52	102	21	43
40	Sudan	292	**115**	170	69	28.1	1099	126	480x	54	46	52	..	..
41	Nepal	290	**114**	190	81	21.9	833	95	200	55	28	109	22x	40x
42	Gambia	375	**110**	213	80	1.1	47	5	330	46	39	67	..	..
43	Senegal	303	**110**	174	70	8.3	350	39	600	50	33	58	11	59
44	Yemen	340	**110**	230	76	14.5	687	76	280	51	39x	78	..	..
45	Congo	220	**108**	143	81	2.6	113	12	620	51	75	..	..	..
46	Cameroon	264	**106**	156	66	13.2	532	56	680	57	63	87	..	..
47	Bolivia	252	**105**	152	73	7.4	257	27	770	60	83	95	15	48
48	Papua New Guinea	248	**95**	165	67	4.3	141	13	1240	57	72	74	..	..
49	Kenya	202	**90**	120	61	28.3	1231	111	250	55	78	91	10	62
50	Turkmenistan	..	**85**	..	69	4.1	124	11	1230x	66	98x	..	18	43
51	Tajikistan	..	**79**	..	61	6.1	214	17	360	71	98x	89	..	..
52	Namibia	206	**78**	129	61	1.5	56	4	1970	60	..	136	..	..
53	Indonesia	216	**75**	127	50	197.6	4716	354	880	64	84	114	21	41
54	Morocco	215	**75**	133	61	27.0	740	56	1140	65	44	73	17	46
55	Mongolia	185	**74**	128	57	2.4	64	5	300	65	83	97	..	..
56	Zimbabwe	181	**74**	109	50	11.3	423	31	500	52	85	119	10	62
57	Iraq	171	**71**	117	57	20.4	762	54	1036x	67	58	91	..	..
58	Guatemala	205	**67**	137	49	10.6	400	27	1200	66	56	85	8x	63x
59	South Africa	126	**67**	89	51	41.5	1260	84	3040	64	82	111	9	63
60	Libyan Arab Jamahiriya	269	**63**	160	52	5.4	222	14	5310x	64	76	110	..	..
61	Uzbekistan	..	**62**	..	50	22.8	680	42	960	70	97x	80	..	..
62	Algeria	243	**61**	148	51	27.9	786	48	1650	68	62	103	18x	46x
63	Brazil	181	**60**	118	51	161.8	3822	229	2970	67	83	111	7x	68x
64	Nicaragua	209	**60**	140	46	4.4	170	10	340	68	66	103	12	55
65	Peru	236	**55**	143	41	23.8	631	35	2110	67	89	119	14	50
66	Kyrgyzstan	..	**54**	..	45	4.7	129	7	630	70	97x	..	10	57
67	Philippines	102	**53**	73	40	67.6	1975	105	950	67	95	111	17x	48x
68	Botswana	170	**52**	117	41	1.5	54	3	2800	66	70	116	11	59
69	Egypt	258	**51**	169	40	62.9	1737	89	720	65	51	97	21	41
70	Azerbaijan	..	**50**	..	34	7.6	157	8	500	71	97x	89	..	..
71	Turkey	217	**50**	161	44	61.9	1609	81	2500	68	82	103	..	..
72	China	209	**47**	140	38	1221.5	21726	1021	530	69	82	118	17	44
73	Kazakstan	..	**47**	..	40	17.1	323	15	1160	70	98x	86	20	40
74	Viet Nam	219	**45**	147	34	74.5	2195	99	200	66	94	111	19	44
75	Dominican Rep.	152	**44**	104	37	7.8	199	9	1330	70	82	97	12x	56x

		Under-5 mortality rate		Infant mortality rate (under 1)		Total population (millions)	Annual no. of births (thousands)	Annual no. of under-5 deaths (thousands)	GNP per capita (US$)	Life expectancy at birth (years)	Total adult literacy rate	Primary school enrolment ratio (gross)	% share of household income 1990-94	
		1960	1995	1960	1995	1995	1995	1995	1994	1995	1995	1990-95	lowest 40%	highest 20%
76	Albania	151	**40**	112	34	3.4	79	3	380	72	..	96	..	..
77	Ecuador	180	**40**	115	31	11.5	309	12	1280	69	90	123	14	53
78	El Salvador	210	**40**	130	34	5.8	189	8	1360	67	72	79	..	..
79	Iran, Islamic Rep. of	233	**40**	145	35	67.3	2261	90	1033x	69	69	105	..	..
80	Lebanon	85	**40**	65	33	3.0	76	3	2150x	69	92	115	..	..
81	Honduras	203	**38**	137	31	5.7	200	8	600	69	73	112	11	57
82	Tunisia	244	**37**	163	30	8.9	215	8	1790	69	67	118	16	46
83	Colombia	132	**36**	82	30	35.1	806	29	1670	70	91	119	11	56
84	Syrian Arab Rep.	201	**36**	136	30	14.7	588	21	1160x	68	71	105	..	..
85	Moldova	..	**34**	..	30	4.4	68	2	870	68	96x	77	19	42
86	Paraguay	90	**34**	66	28	5.0	156	5	1580	71	92	112	..	..
87	Saudi Arabia	292	**34**	170	29	17.9	634	22	7050	71	63	75	..	..
88	Mexico	148	**32**	103	27	93.7	2463	79	4180	71	90	112	12	55
89	Thailand	146	**32**	101	27	58.8	1124	36	2410	69	94	98	14	53
90	Armenia	..	**31**	..	26	3.6	69	2	680	73	99x	90	..	..
91	TFYR Macedonia	177	**31**	120	26	2.2	32	1	820	72	..	87	..	..
92	Korea, Dem. Peo. Rep.	120	**30**	85	23	23.9	558	17	970x	72	..	104x	..	..
93	Russian Federation	..	**30**	..	27	147.0	1519	46	2650	68	98x	109	12	54
94	Romania	82	**29**	69	23	22.8	253	7	1270	70	97x	86	24	35
95	Argentina	68	**27**	57	24	34.6	689	19	8110	73	96	107	..	..
96	Georgia	..	**26**	..	22	5.5	84	2	580x	73	99x	..	..	..
97	Latvia	..	**26**	..	22	2.6	28	1	2320	69	99x	83	23	37
98	Jordan	149	**25**	103	21	5.4	206	5	1440	69	87	94	16	50
99	Oman	300	**25**	180	20	2.2	93	2	5140	70	..	85	..	..
100	Ukraine	..	**24**	..	20	51.4	574	14	1910	69	98x	87	24	35
101	Venezuela	70	**24**	53	20	21.8	570	14	2760	72	91	96	11	58
102	Yugoslavia	120	**23**	87	20	10.8	150	4	a	72	93x	72	..	..
103	Mauritius	84	**23**	62	19	1.1	23	1	3150	71	83	106	..	..
104	Estonia	..	**22**	..	19	1.5	16	1	2820	69	100x	83	17	46
105	Uruguay	47	**21**	41	19	3.2	54	1	4660	73	97	109	..	..
106	Belarus	..	**20**	..	17	10.1	117	2	2160	70	98x	96	26	33
107	Panama	104	**20**	67	18	2.6	62	1	2580	73	91	105	8x	60x
108	Bulgaria	70	**19**	49	16	8.8	90	2	1250	71	98x	86	21	39
109	Lithuania	..	**19**	..	16	3.7	48	1	1350	70	98x	92	20	42
110	Sri Lanka	130	**19**	90	15	18.4	365	7	640	73	90	106	22	39
111	United Arab Emirates	240	**19**	160	16	1.9	41	1	21430x	74	79	110	..	..
112	Trinidad and Tobago	73	**18**	61	16	1.3	26	1	3740	72	98	94	..	..
113	Bosnia and Herzegovina	155	**17**	105	15	3.5	48	1	b	73	..	..	..	..
114	Poland	70	**16**	62	14	38.4	501	8	2410	71	99x	98	23	37
115	Costa Rica	112	**16**	80	14	3.4	86	1	2400	77	95	105	13x	51x
116	Slovakia	..	**15**	..	13	5.4	77	1	2250	71	..	101	28	31
117	Chile	138	**15**	107	13	14.3	299	5	3520	74	95	98	10	61
118	Croatia	98	**14**	70	12	4.5	50	1	2560	72	97x	87	..	..
119	Hungary	57	**14**	51	13	10.1	121	2	3840	69	99x	95	24	37
120	Kuwait	128	**14**	89	12	1.5	40	1	19420	75	79	65	..	..
121	Jamaica	76	**13**	58	11	2.4	50	1	1540	74	85	109	16	48
122	Malaysia	105	**13**	73	11	20.1	543	7	3480	71	84	93	13x	54x
123	Portugal	112	**11**	81	9	9.8	117	1	9320	75	85x	120	..	..
124	Cuba	50	**10**	39	9	11.0	177	2	1170x	76	96	104	..	..
125	United States	30	**10**	26	8	263.3	4041	40	25880	76	..	107	16x	42x
126	Czech Rep.	..	**10**	..	9	10.3	138	1	3200	71	..	* 99	24	37
127	Belgium	35	**10**	31	8	10.1	121	1	22870	77	..	99	22x	36x
128	Greece	64	**10**	53	8	10.5	102	1	7700	78	95x	98	..	..
129	Spain	57	**9**	46	8	39.6	382	4	13440	78	95x	104	22x	37x
130	Korea, Rep. of	124	**9**	88	8	45.0	736	7	8260	72	98	98	20	42
131	France	34	**9**	29	7	58.0	734	7	23420	77	..	106	17x	42x
132	Israel	39	**9**	32	7	5.6	113	1	14530	77	92x	95	18x	40x
133	New Zealand	26	**9**	22	7	3.6	60	1	13350	76	..	102	16x	45x
134	Slovenia	45	**8**	37	7	1.9	20	0	7040	73	..	97	23	38
135	Australia	24	**8**	20	7	18.1	263	2	18000	78	..	108	16x	42x
136	Italy	50	**8**	44	7	57.2	557	4	19300	78	97x	98	19x	41x
137	Netherlands	22	**8**	18	6	15.5	198	2	22010	78	..	97	21x	37x
138	Norway	23	**8**	19	6	4.3	62	1	26390	77	..	99	19x	37x
139	Canada	33	**8**	28	6	29.5	432	3	19510	78	97x	105	18x	40x
140	Austria	43	**7**	37	6	8.0	94	1	24630	77	..	103	..	..
141	United Kingdom	27	**7**	23	6	58.3	773	6	18340	77	..	112	15x	44x
142	Switzerland	27	**7**	22	6	7.2	91	1	37930	78	..	101	17x	45x
143	Ireland	36	**7**	31	6	3.6	52	0	13530	76	..	103	..	..
144	Germany	40	**7**	34	6	81.6	775	5	25580	76	..	97	19x	40x
145	Denmark	25	**7**	22	6	5.2	64	0	27970	76	..	98	17x	39x
146	Japan	40	**6**	31	4	125.1	1278	8	34630	80	..	102	22x	38x
147	Hong Kong*	52	**6**	38	5	5.9	61	0	21650	79	92	102	16x	47x
148	Singapore	40	**6**	31	5	2.8	43	0	22500	75	91	107	15x	49x
149	Finland	28	**5**	22	4	5.1	66	0	18850	76	..	100	18x	38x
150	Sweden	20	**5**	16	4	8.8	123	1	23530	79	..	100	21x	37x

Countries listed in descending order of their 1995 under-five mortality rates (shown in bold type).
a: Range US$726 to US$2895. b: Range US$725 or less.

Table 2: Nutrition

| | | % of infants with low birth weight 1990-94 | % of children (1990-96) who are: | | | % of under-fives (1990-96) suffering from: | | | | Total goitre rate (6-11 years) (%) 1985-94 | % of households consuming iodized salt 1992-96 | Daily per capita calorie supply as a % of requirements 1988-90 |
| | | | exclusively breastfed (0-3 months) | breastfed with complementary food (6-9 months) | still breastfeeding (20-23 months) | underweight | | wasting | stunting | | | |
						moderate & severe	severe	moderate & severe	moderate & severe			
1	Niger	15	1	73	60	36	12	16	32	9	0	95
2	Angola	19	3	83	53	..	..	..	..	7	0	80
3	Sierra Leone	11	..	94	41	29	..	9	35	7	75	83
4	Mozambique	20	..	..	..	27	11	5	55	20	62	77
5	Afghanistan	20	..	..	..	..	..	..	..	20	..	72
6	Guinea-Bissau	20	..	..	..	23x	..	..	..	19	0	97
7	Guinea	21	..	..	..	26	9	12	32	19	..	97
8	Malawi	20	11	78	68	30	9	7	48	13	58	88
9	Liberia	..	15x	17	25	..	..	..	..	6	..	98
10	Somalia	16	..	..	..	..	..	..	..	7	..	81
11	Mali	17	12	39	44x	31x	9x	11x	24x	29	20	96
12	Zambia	13	13	88	34	28	9	6	53	51x	90	87
13	Eritrea	13	65	54	..	41	..	10	66	..	80	..
14	Ethiopia	16	74	39	35	48	16	8	64	22	0	73
15	Mauritania	11	59	39	58	23	9	7	44	..	3	106
16	Nigeria	16	2	52	43	36	12	9	43	10	83	93
17	Bhutan	..	..	..	..	38x	..	4x	56x	25	96	128
18	Uganda	..	70	64	40	23x	5x	2x	45x	7	50	93
19	Zaire	15	32	40	64	34	10	10	45	9	12	96
20	Burundi	..	89x	66x	73x	37	11	9	43	42	80	84
21	Cambodia	..	..	..	..	40	7	8	38	15	0	96
22	Central African Rep.	15	4	93	52	27	8	7	34	63	28	82
23	Burkina Faso	21	3	44	81	30	8	13	29	16	22	94
24	Madagascar	17	47	80	45	34	10	7	50	24	1	95
25	Tanzania , U. Rep. of	14	73	94	48	29	7	6	47	37	74	95
26	Lesotho	11	..	..	..	21	2x	2	33	43	..	93
27	Chad	..	..	..	..	..	..	..	..	15	31	73
28	Côte d'Ivoire	14	3	65	45	24	6	8	24	6	0	111
29	Myanmar	16	30	40	56	43	16	8	45	18	14	114
30	Gabon	..	..	..	..	..	..	..	..	5	..	104
31	Benin	..	..	..	..	..	..	..	..	24x	35	104
32	Rwanda	17	90	68	85	29	6	4	48	49	90	82
33	Pakistan	25	16	31	56	38	13	9	50	32	19	99
34	Lao Peo. Dem. Rep.	18	36	..	31	44	14	10	48	25	..	111
35	Ghana	7	19	63	48	27	8	11	26	10	0	93
36	Togo	20	10x	86x	68x	24x	6x	5x	30x	22	0	99
37	Haiti	15	3	83	25	28	8	8	32	4x	10	89
38	Bangladesh	50	54	30	87	67	25	17	63	11x	44	88
39	India	33	51	31	67	53	21	18	52	9	67	101
40	Sudan	15	14x	45x	44x	34	11	13	34	20	..	87
41	Nepal	..	36	..	..	49	31	6	63	44	68	100
42	Gambia	..	..	..	61	..	..	..	..	..	0	..
43	Senegal	11	7	41	48	20	5	9	22	12	10	98
44	Yemen	19	15	51	31	39	13	13	39	32	21	..
45	Congo	16	43x	95x	27x	24x	3x	4x	21x	8	..	103
46	Cameroon	13	7	77	35	14	3	3	24	26	86	95
47	Bolivia	12	53	78	36	16	4	4	28	21	92	84
48	Papua New Guinea	23	..	..	..	35x	..	..	..	30	..	114
49	Kenya	16	17	90	54	23	6	8	34	7	100	89
50	Turkmenistan	5	54	..	..	..	..	..	..	20	0	..
51	Tajikistan	..	..	..	..	..	..	..	..	20	20	..
52	Namibia	16	22	65	23	26	6	9	28	35	80	..
53	Indonesia	14	47	85	63	35	..	..	..	28	50	121
54	Morocco	9	31	33	20	9	2	2	23	20	..	125
55	Mongolia	6	..	..	..	12	..	2	26	7	..	97
56	Zimbabwe	14	16	93	26	16	3	6	21	42	80	94
57	Iraq	15	..	..	..	12	2	3	22	7	50	128
58	Guatemala	14	50	56	43	27	6	3	50	20	93	103
59	South Africa	..	..	..	..	9	1	3	23	2	40	128
60	Libyan Arab Jamahiriya	..	..	..	..	5	..	3	15	6	90	140
61	Uzbekistan	..	..	..	..	..	..	..	..	18	0	..
62	Algeria	9	48	29	21	13	3	9	18	9	92	123
63	Brazil	11	4x	27x	13x	7x	1x	2x	16x	14x	79	114
64	Nicaragua	15	11	48	17	12	1	2	24	4	79	99
65	Peru	11	40	62	36	11	2	1	37	36	90	87
66	Kyrgyzstan	..	38	50	25	..	..	..	..	20	0	..
67	Philippines	15	33	52	18	30	5	8	33	15	40	104
68	Botswana	8	41x	82x	23x	15x	..	..	44x	8	27	97
69	Egypt	10	68	52	..	9	2	3	24	5	90	132
70	Azerbaijan	..	..	..	..	..	..	..	..	20	..	..
71	Turkey	8	14	17	14	10	2	3	21	36	31	127
72	China	9	64	..	..	16	3x	4	32	9	51	112
73	Kazakstan	..	12	61	21	..	..	..	..	20	14	..
74	Viet Nam	17	10	32	7	45	11	12	47	20	42	103
75	Dominican Rep.	11	10	32	7	10	2	1	19	5	40	102

		% of infants with low birth weight 1990-94	% of children (1990-96) who are:			% of under-fives (1990-96) suffering from:				Total goitre rate (6-11 years) (%) 1985-94	% of households consuming iodized salt 1992-96	Daily per capita calorie supply as a % of requirements 1988-90
			exclusively breastfed (0-3 months)	breastfed with complementary food (6-9 months)	still breastfeeding (20-23 months)	underweight moderate & severe	underweight severe	wasting moderate & severe	stunting moderate & severe			
76	Albania	7								41		107
77	Ecuador	13	29	52	34	17x	0x	2x	34x	10	90	105
78	El Salvador	11	20	71	28	11	1	1	23	25	91	102
79	Iran, Islamic Rep. of	9	53	..	..	16	3	7	19	30	82	125
80	Lebanon	10	..	..	..	..	..			15	92	127
81	Honduras	9	11	..	..	18	3	2	40	9	85	98
82	Tunisia	8	12	53x	16	9	2x	4	22	4x	..	131
83	Colombia	10	16	61	17	8	1	1	15	10	90	106
84	Syrian Arab Rep.	11	..	50	..	12	3	8	27	73	21	126
85	Moldova	4								..	..	..
86	Paraguay	5	7	61	8	4	1	0	17	49	64	116
87	Saudi Arabia	7	..	..	..	..	..	..	..	..	..	121
88	Mexico	8	38x	36x	21x	14x	..	6x	22x	15	87	131
89	Thailand	13	4x	69x	34x	26x	4x	6x	22x	12	50	103
90	Armenia	..	..	..	..	..		..	..	10	..	..
91	TFYR Macedonia	..								..	100	..
92	Korea, Dem. Peo. Rep.	..	..	..	..	..		..	..	..	5	121
93	Russian Federation	..	..	..	..	..		..	..	..	30	..
94	Romania	11	..	..	..	..		..	..	10	..	116
95	Argentina	7	..	..	..	..		..	..	8	90	131
96	Georgia	..								20	..	..
97	Latvia	..								..	..	..
98	Jordan	7	32	48	13	9	1	2	16	..	75	110
99	Oman	8	..	..	..	12	..	..	12	10	..	..
100	Ukraine	..	..	..	..	..		..	..	10	4	..
101	Venezuela	9	..	..	..	6x	..	2x	6x	11	65	99
102	Yugoslavia	..								..	70	..
103	Mauritius	13	16	29	..	16	2	15	10	..	0	128
104	Estonia	..								..	..	..
105	Uruguay	8	..	..	..	7x	2x	..	16x	..	..	101
106	Belarus	..								22	37	..
107	Panama	9	32	38	21	7	1	1	9	13	92	98
108	Bulgaria	6	..	..	..	..		..	..	20	..	148
109	Lithuania	..								..	..	..
110	Sri Lanka	25	24	60	66	38	7	16	24	14	7	101
111	United Arab Emirates	6	..	..	26	..	..	..	..	..	..	..
112	Trinidad and Tobago	10	10x	39x	16x	7x	0x	4x	5x	..	..	114
113	Bosnia and Herzegovina	..	..	..	..	..		..	..	..	..	..
114	Poland	..								10	..	131
115	Costa Rica	6	35	47	12	2	0	2	8	3	91	121
116	Slovakia	..								..	..	..
117	Chile	5	..	..	..	1	..	0	3	9x	90	102
118	Croatia	..								..	100	..
119	Hungary	9	..	..	..	..		..	..	..	..	137
120	Kuwait	7	..	..	..	6x	..	3x	12x	..	..	..
121	Jamaica	10	..	..	..	10	1	4	6	..	100	114
122	Malaysia	8	..	..	..	23	1	..	..	20	..	120
123	Portugal	5	..	..	..	..		..	..	15	..	136
124	Cuba	9	..	..	..	..		1x	..	10	0	135
125	United States	7	..	..	..	..		..	..	..	..	138
126	Czech Rep.	6								..	..	..
127	Belgium	6	..	..	..	..		..	..	5	..	149
128	Greece	6	..	..	..	..		..	..	10	..	151
129	Spain	4	..	..	..	..		..	..	10	..	141
130	Korea, Rep. of	9	..	..	..	..		..	..	..	..	120
131	France	5	..	..	..	..		..	..	5x	..	143
132	Israel	7								..	..	125
133	New Zealand	6	..	..	..	..		..	..	..	..	131
134	Slovenia	..								..	..	..
135	Australia	6	..	..	..	..		..	..	..	..	124
136	Italy	5	..	..	..	..		..	..	20	..	139
137	Netherlands	..								3	..	114
138	Norway	4	..	..	..	..		..	..	..	..	120
139	Canada	6	..	..	..	..		..	..	..	..	122
140	Austria	6								..	..	133
141	United Kingdom	7	..	..	..	..		..	..	..	..	130
142	Switzerland	5	..	..	..	..		..	..	..	..	130
143	Ireland	4	..	..	..	..		..	..	..	..	157
144	Germany	..								10	..	..
145	Denmark	6	..	..	..	..		..	..	5	..	135
146	Japan	7								..	..	125
147	Hong Kong*	8	..	..	..	..		..	..	..	..	125
148	Singapore	7	..	..	..	..		..	..	..	..	136
149	Finland	4	..	..	..	..		..	..	..	..	113
150	Sweden	5	..	..	..	..		..	..	..	..	111

Countries listed in descending order of their 1995 under-five mortality rates (table 1).

Table 3: Health

#		% of population with access to safe water 1990-96			% of population with access to adequate sanitation 1990-96			% of population with access to health services 1990-95			% fully immunized 1992-95 1-year-old children				pregnant women tetanus	ORT use rate 1990-96
		total	urban	rural	total	urban	rural	total	urban	rural	TB	DPT	polio	measles		
1	Niger	54	46	55	15	71	4	99	32	..	32	18	18	18	57	20
2	Angola	32	69	15	16	34	8	..	..	..	40	21	23	32	14	..
3	Sierra Leone	34	58	21	11	17	8	38	90	20	60	43	43	46	61	
4	Mozambique	63	..	..	54	..	..	39x	100x	30x	58	46	46	40	61	83
5	Afghanistan	12	39	5	..	13	..	29x	80x	17x	31	41	56	41	3	..
6	Guinea-Bissau	59	32	67	30	24	32	40	..	..	100	100	98	82	53	
7	Guinea	55	50	56	21	84	10	80	100	70	86	73	73	69	56	38
8	Malawi	37	80	32	6	22	4	35	81	29	91	76	80	70	77	78
9	Liberia	46	79	13	30	56	4	39x	50x	30x	92	62	62	68	77	94
10	Somalia	31	..	28	12	6	2	..	..	..	37	28	28	45	11	97
11	Mali	45	46	43	31	58	21	40	..	..	75	46	46	49	19	..
12	Zambia	27	50	17	64	89	43	..	..	..	63	72	72	69	44	99
13	Eritrea	..	..	7	..	..	..	..	..	..	57	45	45	45	19	38
14	Ethiopia	25	91	19	19	97	7	46	..	..	63	51	48	43	22	95
15	Mauritania	66x	67x	65x	..	34x	..	63	..	..	93	50	50	53	28	31
16	Nigeria	51	84	40	58	84	48	51	..	..	57	27	27	40	21	..
17	Bhutan	58	75	54	70	90	66	65x	..	..	98	87	86	85	70	85
18	Uganda	38	60	35	64	96	47	49	99	42	98	79	78	79	76	46
19	Zaire	42	89	26	18	53	6	26x	40x	17x	46	26	27	39	33	90
20	Burundi	59	93	54	51	60	51	80	100	79	77	63	62	50	30	..
21	Cambodia	36	65	33	14	81	8	53x	80x	50x	95	79	80	75	36	..
22	Central African Rep.	38	59	23	52	83	36	52	89	30	73	38	37	36	50	34
23	Burkina Faso	78	..	..	18	42	11	90	100	89	78	47	47	55	39	100
24	Madagascar	29	83	10	3	12	3	38	81	19	77	64	63	60	33	85
25	Tanzania , U. Rep. of	38	73	29	86	96	84	42	..	..	92	88	86	82	71	76
26	Lesotho	56	44	58	28	42	25	80x	..	..	59	58	59	74	12	42
27	Chad	24	48	17	21	73	7	30	64	..	36	17	16	26	50	..
28	Côte d'Ivoire	75	..	..	43	..	..	..	..	..	48	40	40	57	22	18
29	Myanmar	60	78	50	43	56	36	60	100	47	82	72	72	75	83	96
30	Gabon	68x	90x	50x	..	..	..	..	..	..	73	56	57	56	29	..
31	Benin	50	41	53	20	54	6	18x	..	..	91	79	79	72	77	60
32	Rwanda	..	..	79	..	..	85	80	..	..	86	57	57	50	88	47
33	Pakistan	74	82	69	47	77	22	55x	99x	35x	75	35	37	53	36	97
34	Lao Peo. Dem. Rep.	52	60	51	28	98	16	67x	..	..	59	53	64	68	35	..
35	Ghana	65	88	52	55	62	44	60x	92x	45x	70	55	55	46	64	93
36	Togo	63	74	58	23	56	10	..	80	..	81	73	71	65	43	..
37	Haiti	28	37	23	24	42	16	60	..	39	68	34	34	31	49	31
38	Bangladesh	97	99	96	48	79	44	45	..	..	94	69	69	79	78	96
39	India	81	85	79	29	70	14	85	100	80	96	89	98	78	79	31
40	Sudan	60	84	41	22	79	4	70	..	..	88	76	77	74	65	..
41	Nepal	63	88	60	18	58	12	..	..	..	61	63	62	57	11	27
42	Gambia	48	67	..	37	51	50	93	..	..	98	90	92	87	93	..
43	Senegal	52	85	28	58	83	40	90	100	85	90	80	80	80	39	18
44	Yemen	61	88	55	24	47	17	38	81	32	87	37	36	40	3	92
45	Congo	34	53	7	69	..	..	83x	97x	70x	94	79	79	70	75	41
46	Cameroon	50	57	43	50	64	36	80	96	69	54	46	46	46	12	..
47	Bolivia	66	87	36	55	72	32	67	77	52	85	85	86	80	65	43
48	Papua New Guinea	28	84	17	22	82	11	96x	..	..	78	50	55	63	31	..
49	Kenya	53	67	49	77	69	81	77	..	..	92	84	84	73	72	76
50	Turkmenistan	74	..	..	90	..	..	100	..	..	88	80	83	66	..	98
51	Tajikistan	..	82	49	..	46	..	..	..	..	96	93	96	80	..	66
52	Namibia	57	87	42	34	77	12	59	87	42	94	76	74	69	72	66
53	Indonesia	62	79	54	51	73	40	93	99	91	86	78	79	70	74	99
54	Morocco	55	94	18	41	69	18	70x	100x	50x	93	90	90	88	37	29
55	Mongolia	80	100	58	74	100	47	95x	..	..	94	88	86	85	..	..
56	Zimbabwe	77	99	64	66	99	48	85	96	80	95	80	80	74	46	60
57	Iraq	78	92	44	70	85	37	93x	97x	78x	99	91	91	95	72	..
58	Guatemala	64	87	49	59	72	52	57	..	..	78	59	56	75	55	22
59	South Africa	99	99	53	53	85	12	..	..	..	95	73	72	76	26	..
60	Libyan Arab Jamahiriya	97	97	97	98	99	94	95	100	85	99	96	96	92	45	49
61	Uzbekistan	62	82	49	22	46	..	..	..	..	95	89	99	81	..	98
62	Algeria	78	91	64	91	99	80	98	100	95	93	83	83	77	52	98
63	Brazil	73	85	69	44	55	4	..	..	..	100	83	83	88	70	..
64	Nicaragua	53	84	29	60	77	34	83x	100x	60x	100	85	96	81	49	54
65	Peru	72	75	18	57	58	25	44	..	..	96	95	93	98	21	92
66	Kyrgyzstan	..	84	..	30	60	10	..	..	..	90	82	81	80	..	98
67	Philippines	86	92	80	77	88	66	71	..	..	91	85	86	86	48	63
68	Botswana	93x	100x	91x	55	91	41	..	..	..	81	78	78	68	56	..
69	Egypt	79	..	..	32	..	..	99	100	99	95	90	91	90	64	43
70	Azerbaijan										93	93	98	97		
71	Turkey	80	91	59	..	..	..	..	..	..	42	51	51	42	38	16
72	China	67	97	56	24	74	7	88	100	83	92	92	94	93	11	85
73	Kazakstan										89	93	95	..		
74	Viet Nam	43	47	42	22	47	16	90	100	80	96	93	94	95	82	..
75	Dominican Rep.	65	80	..	78	76	83	78	84	67	74	83	80	85	52	..

		% of population with access to safe water 1990-96			% of population with access to adequate sanitation 1990-96			% of population with access to health services 1990-95			% fully immunized 1992-95 — 1-year-old children				pregnant women tetanus	ORT use rate 1990-96
		total	urban	rural	total	urban	rural	total	urban	rural	TB	DPT	polio	measles		
76	Albania	..	..	..	..	..	..	..	..	..	97	97	98	91	..	..
77	Ecuador	68	80	49	76	95	49	..	70x	20x	91	72	70	62	21	64
78	El Salvador	69	85	46	81	91	65	40	..	..	100	100	94	93	80	69
79	Iran, Islamic Rep. of	90	98	82	81	86	74	88	100	75	99	97	97	95	82	37
80	Lebanon	94	96	88	63	81	8	95	98	85	..	92	92	88	..	82
81	Honduras	87	96	79	87	97	78	69	86	55	99	96	96	90	48	32
82	Tunisia	98	100	95	80	96	52	..	..	..	89	92	92	91	49	..
83	Colombia	85	97	56	85	97	56	81	86	72	99	93	95	84	57	45
84	Syrian Arab Rep.	85	92	78	83	84	82	90	96	84	100	100	100	98	76	36
85	Moldova	55	98	18	50	90	8	..	..	..	98	96	99	98	..	..
86	Paraguay	42	70	10	41	65	14	63x	90x	38x	92	79	79	75	66	33
87	Saudi Arabia	95x	100x	74x	86x	100x	30x	97x	100x	88x	93	97	97	94	62	58
88	Mexico	83	92	57	72	85	32	93	..	..	98	92	92	90	42	81
89	Thailand	89	94	88	96	98	95	90x	90x	90x	98	94	94	90	93	95
90	Armenia	..	..	..	..	..	..	..	..	..	83	83	92	95	..	..
91	TFYR Macedonia	..	..	..	..	..	..	..	..	..	96	88	91	86	91	..
92	Korea, Dem. Peo. Rep.	..	..	..	..	..	..	..	..	..	99	96	99	98	95	..
93	Russian Federation	..	..	..	..	..	..	..	..	..	96	93	92	94	..	..
94	Romania	..	..	..	..	..	..	..	..	..	100	98	94	93	..	..
95	Argentina	71	77	29	68	73	37	71x	80x	21x	96	66	70	76	..	..
96	Georgia	..	..	..	..	..	..	..	..	..	30	58	82	63	..	..
97	Latvia	..	..	..	..	..	..	..	..	..	100	65	70	85	..	..
98	Jordan	98	..	..	77	..	..	97x	98x	95x	..	100	99	92	59	41
99	Oman	82	..	..	78	..	..	96	100	94	96	99	99	98	95	85
100	Ukraine	..	..	..	..	..	..	..	..	..	92	94	95	96	..	..
101	Venezuela	79	80	75	59	64	30	..	..	..	91	68	85	67	18	..
102	Yugoslavia	..	..	..	..	..	..	..	..	..	68	92	93	81	..	..
103	Mauritius	99	95	100	99	99	99	100x	100x	100x	87	89	89	85	78	..
104	Estonia	..	..	..	..	..	..	..	..	..	99	84	89	81	..	..
105	Uruguay	75x	85x	5x	61x	60x	65x	82x	..	..	99	86	86	80	13	..
106	Belarus	..	..	..	..	..	..	..	..	..	93	90	93	97	..	..
107	Panama	93	..	..	83	..	..	70	..	..	100	86	86	84	24	94
108	Bulgaria	..	..	..	..	..	..	..	..	..	98	100	94	93	..	..
109	Lithuania	..	..	..	..	..	..	..	..	..	97	96	89	94	..	..
110	Sri Lanka	57	88	52	63	68	62	..	..	..	90	93	92	88	81	34
111	United Arab Emirates	95	..	..	77	93	22	99	..	..	98	90	90	90	..	..
112	Trinidad and Tobago	97	99	91	79	99	98	100	100	99	..	89	90	84	19	..
113	Bosnia and Herzegovina	..	..	..	..	..	..	..	..	..	85	67	69	57	..	..
114	Poland	..	..	..	..	..	..	..	..	..	94	95	95	91	..	..
115	Costa Rica	96	100	92	84	95	70	..	..	..	99	85	86	94	90	31
116	Slovakia	..	..	..	..	..	..	..	..	..	98	99	98	99	..	..
117	Chile	..	98	81	..	86	..	97x	..	..	96	92	92	96	..	..
118	Croatia	..	..	..	..	..	..	..	..	..	98	90	90	92	93	..
119	Hungary	..	..	..	..	..	..	..	..	..	100	100	100	100	..	..
120	Kuwait	..	..	..	..	100x	..	100x	..	..	..	100	100	93	21	..
121	Jamaica	86	..	..	89	100	80	90x	..	..	100	92	92	89	82	..
122	Malaysia	78	96	66	94	..	..	..	..	..	97	90	90	81	79	..
123	Portugal	..	..	..	..	..	..	..	..	..	94	93	95	94	..	..
124	Cuba	89	96	69	92	95	82	100	..	..	99	100	93	100	61	..
125	United States	..	..	..	..	..	..	..	..	..	..	94	84	89	..	..
126	Czech Rep.	..	..	..	..	..	..	..	..	..	..	96	98	96	..	..
127	Belgium	..	..	..	..	..	..	..	..	..	..	97	94	70	..	..
128	Greece	..	..	..	..	..	..	..	..	..	50	78	95	70	..	..
129	Spain	..	..	..	..	..	..	..	..	..	..	88	88	90	..	..
130	Korea, Rep. of	93	100	76	100	100	100	100	100	100	93	93	93	92	..	..
131	France	..	..	..	..	..	..	..	..	..	78	89	92	76	..	..
132	Israel	..	..	..	..	..	..	..	..	..	..	92	93	94	..	..
133	New Zealand	97	100	82	..	..	..	..	..	..	20	84	84	87	..	..
134	Slovenia	..	..	..	..	..	..	..	..	..	99	98	98	91	..	..
135	Australia	..	..	..	..	..	..	..	..	..	..	..	..	..	..	..
136	Italy	..	..	..	..	..	..	..	..	..	..	50	98	50	..	..
137	Netherlands	..	..	..	..	..	..	..	..	..	..	97	97	95	..	..
138	Norway	..	..	..	..	..	..	..	..	..	..	92	92	93	..	..
139	Canada	..	..	..	..	..	..	..	..	..	..	93	89	98	..	..
140	Austria	..	..	..	..	..	..	..	..	..	..	90	90	60	..	..
141	United Kingdom	..	..	..	..	..	..	..	..	..	..	92	94	92	..	..
142	Switzerland	..	..	..	..	..	..	..	..	..	..	..	..	..	..	..
143	Ireland	..	..	..	..	..	..	..	..	..	..	..	..	..	..	..
144	Germany	..	..	..	..	..	..	..	..	..	..	45	80	75	..	..
145	Denmark	..	..	..	..	..	..	..	..	..	..	89	100	88	..	..
146	Japan	97	100	85	..	85	..	..	..	..	91	85	91	68	..	..
147	Hong Kong*	100	100	96	..	..	..	..	..	..	100	83	84	77	..	..
148	Singapore	100x	100x	..	..	..	..	..	..	..	97	95	93	88	..	..
149	Finland	..	..	..	..	..	..	..	..	..	100	100	100	98	..	..
150	Sweden	..	..	..	..	..	..	..	..	..	..	99	99	96	..	..

Countries listed in descending order of their 1995 under-five mortality rates (table 1).

Table 4: Education

| | | Adult literacy rate | | | | No. of sets per 1000 population 1993 | | Primary school enrolment ratio | | | | | | % of primary school children reaching grade 5 1990-95 | Secondary school enrolment ratio 1990-94 (gross) | |
| | | 1980 | | 1995 | | | | 1960 (gross) | | 1990-94 (gross) | | 1990-95 (net) | | | | |
		male	female	male	female	radio	television	male	female	male	female	male	female		male	female
1	Niger	14	3	21	7	61	5	8	3	35	21	32	18	82	9	4
2	Angola	16x	7x	56x	29x	29	7	30	14	95	87	..	..	34	..	..
3	Sierra Leone	30	9	45	18	233	11	30	15	60	42	..	..	..	22	12
4	Mozambique	44	12	58	23	48	4	71	43	69	51	46	35	35	9	6
5	Afghanistan	33	6	47	15	118	10	14	2	46	16	42	14	43x	22	8
6	Guinea-Bissau	53	26	68	43	40	..	35	15	77x	42x	58x	32x	20x	9x	4x
7	Guinea	34	11	50	22	43	8	27	9	61	30	36x	18x	80	17	6
8	Malawi	64	28	72	42	226	..	50	26	84	77	50	54	37	6	3
9	Liberia	38	11	54	22	227	19	40	13	51x	28x	..	..	..	31x	12x
10	Somalia	8x	1x	36x	14x	41	13	6	2	15x	8x	11x	6x	..	9x	5x
11	Mali	20	9	39	23	44	1	13	5	38	24	23	14	85	12	6
12	Zambia	65	43	86	71	82	27	61	40	100x	92x	82x	80x	..	25x	14x
13	Eritrea	..	..	..	..	..	..	..	..	52	41	27	24	79	17	13
14	Ethiopia	32	14	46	25	197	3	9	3	27	19	33x	24x	58	12	11
15	Mauritania	41	19	50	26	147	23	12	3	76	62	..	..	72	19	11
16	Nigeria	47	23	67	47	196	38	54	31	105	82	..	..	92	32	27
17	Bhutan	41	15	56	28	17	..	5	..	31x	19x	..	..	82	7x	2x
18	Uganda	62	32	74	50	107	11	39	18	74	59	58x	51x	55	14	8
19	Zaire	75	45	87	68	97	2	89	32	78	58	60	47	64	33	15
20	Burundi	37	12	49	23	62	2	33	10	76	62	56	47	74	8	5
21	Cambodia	74x	23x	48x	22x	108	8	..	..	..	55x	..	..	50	..	..
22	Central African Rep.	41	19	69	52	72	5	50	11	88x	55x	71x	46x	65x	17x	6x
23	Burkina Faso	19	4	30	9	27	6	12	5	47	30	38	24	61	11	6
24	Madagascar	56x	43x	88x	73x	192	20	74	57	75	72	64x	63x	28	14	14
25	Tanzania , U. Rep. of	66	34	79	57	26	2	33	16	71	69	50	51	83	6	5
26	Lesotho	71	45	81	62	32	7	73	109	90	105	59	71	60	22	31
27	Chad	47	19	62	35	245	1	29	4	80	38	52x	23x	46	13	2
28	Côte d'Ivoire	34	14	50	30	143	60	62	22	80	58	..	..	73	33	17
29	Myanmar	86	68	89	78	82	3	60	53	107	104	..	..	..	23	23
30	Gabon	54	28	74	53	147	38	..	..	..	..	..	..	50x	..	..
31	Benin	28	10	49	26	91	6	39	15	88	44	71	35	55	17	7
32	Rwanda	55	30	70	52	66	..	65	29	78	76	71	71	60	11	9
33	Pakistan	38	15	50	24	88	18	39	11	57	30	..	..	48	28	13
34	Lao Peo. Dem. Rep.	56	28	69	44	126	7	43	20	123	92	75	61	53	31	19
35	Ghana	59	31	76	54	269	16	58	31	83	70	..	..	80	44	28
36	Togo	49	18	67	37	211	7	64	25	122	81	80	58	50	34	12
37	Haiti	36	29	48	42	48	5	50	39	58	54	25	26	47	22	21
38	Bangladesh	41	17	49	26	47	6	80	31	84	73	74	66	47x	25	13
39	India	55	25	66	38	80	40	83	44	113	91	..	..	62	59	38
40	Sudan	43	17	58	35	257	80	29	11	59	45	..	..	94	24	19
41	Nepal	31	7	41	14	35	3	19	3	130	87	80x	41x	52	46	23
42	Gambia	37	13	53	25	162	..	..	..	79	56	64	46	87	25	13
43	Senegal	31	12	43	23	116	37	37	18	67	50	55	42	88x	21	11
44	Yemen	14x	3x	53x	26x	30	28	..	..	111	43	..	..	..	47	10
45	Congo	65	40	83	67	115	7	..	..	..	..	..	..	53	..	..
46	Cameroon	59	30	75	52	146	25	77	37	109	93	81x	71x	66	32	23
47	Bolivia	81	59	91	76	669	113	70	43	99	90	95	87	60	40	34
48	Papua New Guinea	70	45	81	63	75	3	24	15	80	67	79x	67x	71	15	10
49	Kenya	72	44	86	70	87	11	62	29	92	91	92x	89x	77	28	23
50	Turkmenistan	..	..	99x	97x	..	..	..	..	..	..	..	..	..	..	..
51	Tajikistan	..	..	99x	97x	..	..	..	..	91	88	..	..	..	98	101
52	Namibia	..	..	..	..	140	23	..	..	134	138	86	93	82	49	61
53	Indonesia	78	58	90	78	148	62	78	58	116	112	99	95	92	48	39
54	Morocco	42	16	57	31	219	79	69	28	85	60	73	53	80	40	29
55	Mongolia	82	63	89	77	136	41	80	80	95	100	..	..	..	85x	97x
56	Zimbabwe	83	68	90	80	86	27	82	65	123	114	..	..	76	51	40
57	Iraq	55	25	71	45	217	75	94	36	98	83	83	74	72x	53	34
58	Guatemala	56	41	63	49	68	53	48	39	89	78	..	..	..	25	23
59	South Africa	77	75	82	82	314	101	..	..	111	110	90	93	76	71	84
60	Libyan Arab Jamahiriya	73	31	88	63	226	100	..	..	110	110	98	96	..	95	95
61	Uzbekistan	..	..	98x	96x	..	..	..	..	80	79	..	..	..	96	92
62	Algeria	55	24	74	49	236	79	55	37	111	96	99	89	92	66	55
63	Brazil	76	73	83	83	390	209	58	56	101x	97x	..	..	70	31x	36x
64	Nicaragua	61	61	65	67	261	67	57	59	101	105	79	81	54	39	44
65	Peru	89	71	95	83	253	99	98	74	123x	118x	..	..	..	66x	60x
66	Kyrgyzstan	..	..	98x	96x	..	..	..	..	..	..	..	..	..	..	..
67	Philippines	91	89	95	94	143	47	98	93	108x	107x	97x	96x	67	64x	65x
68	Botswana	70	43	81	60	119	17	38	43	113	120	93	100	84	49	55
69	Egypt	54	26	64	39	307	113	79	52	105	89	95	82	98	81	69
70	Azerbaijan	..	..	99x	96x	..	..	..	..	91	87	..	..	..	89	88
71	Turkey	81	50	92	72	162	176	90	58	107	98	..	..	89	74	48
72	China	79	53	90	73	184	38	131	90	120	116	97	95	88	60	51
73	Kazakhstan	..	..	99x	96x	..	..	..	..	86	86	..	..	..	89	91
74	Viet Nam	90	78	97	91	104	42	103	74	106x	100x	..	..	..	44x	41x
75	Dominican Rep.	75	74	82	82	172	90	75	74	95	99	79	83	58	30	43

| | | Adult literacy rate | | | | No. of sets per 1000 population 1993 | | Primary school enrolment ratio | | | | | | % of primary school children reaching grade 5 1990-95 | Secondary school enrolment ratio 1990-94 (gross) | |
| | | 1980 | | 1995 | | | | 1960 (gross) | | 1990-94 (gross) | | 1990-95(net) | | | | |
		male	female	male	female	radio	television	male	female	male	female	male	female		male	female
76	Albania	..	..	..	..	177	89	102	86	95	97	..	..	92	84	72
77	Ecuador	86	79	92	88	326	88	82	75	124	122	..	..	67x	54	56
78	El Salvador	66	60	74	70	413	94	59	56	79	80	70	71	58	27	30
79	Iran, Islamic Rep. of	61	37	78	59	230	63	59	28	109	101	100	93	90	74	58
80	Lebanon	91	82	95	90	887	346	112	105	117	114	..	..	..	73	78
81	Honduras	64	61	73	73	408	78	68	67	111	112	89	91	..	29	37
82	Tunisia	61	32	79	55	198	81	88	43	123	113	94	89	92	55	49
83	Colombia	87	87	91	91	177	118	74	74	118	120	..	..	59	57	68
84	Syrian Arab Rep.	72	34	86	56	257	62	89	39	111	99	100	91	92	52	42
85	Moldova	..	..	99x	94x	..	..	..	..	78	77	..	..	..	67	72
86	Paraguay	90	84	94	91	170	83	106	94	114	110	97	96	76	36	38
87	Saudi Arabia	60	32	72	50	293	255	32	3	78	73	65	57	94	54	43
88	Mexico	86	80	92	87	255	150	80	75	114	110	..	..	84	57	58
89	Thailand	92	84	96	92	189	113	97	88	98	97	..	..	88	38	37
90	Armenia	..	..	99x	98x	..	..	..	..	87	93	..	..	..	80	90
91	TFYR Macedonia	..	..	..	..	180	165	..	..	88	87	85	84	95	53	55
92	Korea, Dem. Peo. Rep.	..	..	..	..	124	19	..	..	108x	101x	..	..	..	..	..
93	Russian Federation	..	..	100x	98x	338	372	..	..	109	108	94	94	..	84	91
94	Romania	98x	93x	99x	95x	202	200	101	95	87	86	77	76	93	83	82
95	Argentina	94	94	96	96	672	220	99	99	108	107	95	95	..	70	75
96	Georgia	..	..	99x	98x	..	..	..	..	..	..	..	..	..	..	..
97	Latvia	..	..	100x	99x	651	460	..	..	83	82	82	80	..	84	90
98	Jordan	82	54	93	79	243	76	..	..	94	95	89	89	98	52	54
99	Oman	..	..	71	46	580	653	..	..	87	82	74	72	96	64	57
100	Ukraine	..	..	99x	97x	809	339	..	..	87	87	..	..	..	65	95
101	Venezuela	86	82	92	90	443	163	98	99	95	97	87	90	78	29	41
102	Yugoslavia	..	..	98x	89x	207	179	..	..	72	73	69	70	..	64	65
103	Mauritius	82	67	87	79	366	222	96	90	107	106	94	94	100	58	60
104	Estonia	..	..	100x	100x	449x	361	..	..	84	83	79	79	100	87	96
105	Uruguay	94	95	97	98	604	232	117	117	109	108	94	95	94	61x	62x
106	Belarus	..	..	99x	97x	313	272	..	..	96	95	..	..	99	89	96
107	Panama	86	85	91	90	227	169	89	86	108	104	91	92	82	60	65
108	Bulgaria	..	..	99x	97x	450	260	94	92	87	84	83	81	93	66	70
109	Lithuania	..	..	99x	98x	385	383	..	..	95	90	..	..	94	76	79
110	Sri Lanka	91	80	93	87	201	49	107	95	106	105	..	..	92	71	78
111	United Arab Emirates	72	64	79	80	311	106	..	..	112	108	100	99	99	84	94
112	Trinidad and Tobago	97	93	99	97	489	317	111	108	94	94	88	88	95	74	78
113	Bosnia and Herzegovina	..	..	..	..	..	..	..	..	..	..	..	..	..	..	..
114	Poland	99x	97x	99x	98x	439	298	110	107	98	97	96	96	100	82	87
115	Costa Rica	92	91	95	95	258	142	94	92	106	105	87	88	88	45	49
116	Slovakia	..	..	..	..	567	474	..	..	101	101	..	..	97	87	90
117	Chile	92	91	95	95	345	211	87	86	99	98	88	87	95	65	70
118	Croatia	..	..	99x	95x	301	338	..	..	87	87	80	80	98	80	86
119	Hungary	98x	98x	99x	98x	617	427	103	100	95	95	91	92	98	79	82
120	Kuwait	73	59	82	75	408	346	132	99	65	65	46	44	99	60	60
121	Jamaica	73	81	81	89	433	141	78	79	109	108	100	100	96	62	70
122	Malaysia	80	60	89	78	430	151	108	79	93	93	..	..	98	56	61
123	Portugal	78x	65x	89x	81x	232	190	132	129	122	118	100	100	..	63	74
124	Cuba	91	87	96	95	346	170	109	110	104	104	99	100	95	73	81
125	United States	99x	99x	..	..	2120	816	..	..	107	106	99	100	..	98	97
126	Czech Rep.	..	..	..	..	631	476	..	..	99	100	..	..	98	85	88
127	Belgium	99x	99x	..	..	771	453	111	108	99	100	95	97	..	103	104
128	Greece	93x	76x	98x	93x	416	202	104	101	97	98	93	94	100	100	98
129	Spain	94x	86x	97x	93x	311	400	106	116	104	105	99	100	96	107	120
130	Korea, Rep. of	97	90	99	97	1013	215	108	94	97	99	95	97	100	97	96
131	France	99x	98x	..	..	890	412	144	143	107	105	99	99	96	104	107
132	Israel	93x	83x	95x	89x	478	272	99	97	95	96	..	..	100	84	91
133	New Zealand	..	..	..	..	935	451	110	106	102	101	99	98	94	103	104
134	Slovenia	..	..	..	..	377	297	..	..	97	97	..	..	100	88	90
135	Australia	..	..	..	..	1290	489	103	103	108	107	98	99	99	83	86
136	Italy	95x	92x	98x	96x	802	429	112	109	98	99	..	..	100	81	82
137	Netherlands	..	..	..	..	907	491	105	104	96	99	92	96	..	126	120
138	Norway	..	..	..	..	798	427	100	100	99	99	99	99	100	118	114
139	Canada	..	..	..	..	992	618	108	105	106	104	98	97	97	104	103
140	Austria	..	..	..	..	618	479	106	104	103	103	89	91	97	109	104
141	United Kingdom	..	..	..	..	1146	435	92	92	112	113	95	96	..	91	94
142	Switzerland	..	..	..	..	832	400	118	118	100	102	93	95	100	93	89
143	Ireland	..	..	..	..	636	301	107	112	103	103	89	90	100	101	110
144	Germany	..	..	..	..	890	559	..	..	97	98	80	83	100	101	100
145	Denmark	..	..	..	..	1035	538	103	103	97	98	97	98	100	112	115
146	Japan	100x	99x	..	..	911	618	103	102	102	102	100	100	100	95	97
147	Hong Kong*	94	77	96	88	671	286	88	72	106x	105x	95x	96x	..	69x	73x
148	Singapore	92	74	96	86	644	381	120	101	109x	107x	100x	100x	100x	69x	71x
149	Finland	..	..	..	..	996	504	100	95	100	100	..	..	100	110	130
150	Sweden	..	..	..	..	879	470	95	96	100	100	100	99	98	99	100

Countries listed in descending order of their 1995 under-five mortality rates (table1).

Table 5: Demographic indicators

		Population (millions) 1995		Population annual growth rate (%)		Crude death rate		Crude birth rate		Life expectancy		Total fertility rate 1995	% of population urbanized 1995	Average annual growth rate of urban population (%)	
		under 18	under 5	1965-80	1980-95	1960	1995	1960	1995	1960	1995			1965-80	1980-95
1	Niger	5.0	1.9	2.8	3.3	29	18	54	52	36	48	7.3	17	6.8	5.4
2	Angola	5.9	2.2	2.0	3.1	31	18	49	50	33	48	6.9	32	5.5	5.9
3	Sierra Leone	2.3	0.8	1.9	2.2	33	24	48	48	32	40	6.3	36	5.0	4.8
4	Mozambique	8.2	2.9	2.5	1.9	26	18	47	44	38	47	6.3	34	9.5	8.3
5	Afghanistan	9.4	3.6	1.9	1.5	30	21	52	52	34	45	6.6	20	5.3	3.1
6	Guinea-Bissau	0.5	0.2	2.8	2.0	29	20	40	42	35	45	5.6	22	3.9	3.8
7	Guinea	3.6	1.3	1.6	2.7	31	19	53	49	34	46	6.8	30	4.9	5.6
8	Malawi	5.9	2.1	2.9	3.9	28	20	54	49	38	45	6.9	14	7.1	6.5
9	Liberia	1.6	0.6	3.0	3.2	25	13	50	46	42	56	6.6	45	6.1	4.9
10	Somalia	5.0	1.8	3.1	2.1	28	18	50	50	36	48	6.8	26	3.9	3.1
11	Mali	5.8	2.1	2.2	3.0	29	18	52	49	35	47	6.9	27	4.8	5.5
12	Zambia	5.1	1.7	3.1	3.3	23	16	50	43	42	48	5.7	43	6.6	3.9
13	Eritrea	1.8	0.6	2.6	2.6	25	14	49	42	39	52	5.6	17	4.8	4.2
14	Ethiopia	29.0	10.5	2.4	2.8	28	17	51	47	36	49	6.8	13	4.5	4.4
15	Mauritania	1.1	0.4	2.3	2.6	26	14	46	39	39	53	5.2	54	10.1	6.7
16	Nigeria	58.0	20.6	2.6	2.9	24	15	52	44	40	51	6.2	39	5.7	5.4
17	Bhutan	0.8	0.3	1.9	1.9	26	15	42	39	38	52	5.7	6	4.1	5.2
18	Uganda	11.8	4.4	3.3	3.2	21	20	50	50	43	44	7.0	13	5.3	5.6
19	Zaire	23.9	8.6	2.9	3.2	23	14	47	46	42	52	6.5	29	3.5	3.3
20	Burundi	3.4	1.2	1.7	2.9	23	15	46	44	42	51	6.5	8	6.2	6.6
21	Cambodia	5.1	1.8	0.4	3.0	21	13	45	40	42	53	5.1	21	1.3	6.5
22	Central African Rep.	1.6	0.6	2.1	2.4	26	16	43	41	39	50	5.5	39	4.0	3.2
23	Burkina Faso	5.3	1.9	2.3	2.6	28	18	49	46	36	47	6.3	27	5.5	10.4
24	Madagascar	7.8	2.6	2.6	3.3	24	11	49	43	41	58	5.9	27	5.2	5.9
25	Tanzania , U. Rep. of	15.6	5.3	3.0	3.1	23	14	51	42	41	52	5.7	24	9.9	6.5
26	Lesotho	1.0	0.3	2.2	2.8	24	9	43	36	43	62	5.0	23	7.1	6.6
27	Chad	3.2	1.1	2.0	2.3	30	17	46	43	35	49	5.7	21	6.9	3.2
28	Côte d'Ivoire	7.9	2.9	4.0	3.7	25	15	53	49	39	50	7.1	44	6.7	5.2
29	Myanmar	20.2	6.5	2.2	2.1	21	11	42	32	44	59	4.0	26	3.1	2.7
30	Gabon	0.6	0.2	3.3	3.3	24	15	31	38	41	55	5.5	50	6.7	5.5
31	Benin	2.9	1.1	2.4	3.0	33	17	47	48	35	48	6.9	31	7.1	4.5
32	Rwanda	4.2	1.4	3.2	2.9	22	17	50	44	43	47	6.3	6	6.8	4.5
33	Pakistan	70.8	24.0	2.7	3.3	23	9	49	39	44	63	5.9	35	3.8	4.7
34	Lao Peo. Dem. Rep.	2.5	0.9	1.8	2.8	23	14	45	43	40	52	6.4	22	5.1	6.0
35	Ghana	9.0	3.0	2.1	3.2	19	11	48	41	45	57	5.7	36	3.3	4.3
36	Togo	2.2	0.8	3.2	3.1	26	12	48	43	40	56	6.3	31	7.9	5.0
37	Haiti	3.3	1.1	1.7	2.0	23	11	42	35	43	58	4.7	32	3.7	3.9
38	Bangladesh	55.9	17.4	2.8	2.1	22	11	47	35	40	57	4.1	18	6.7	5.3
39	India	384.9	117.4	2.2	2.0	21	9	43	28	44	62	3.6	27	3.6	3.0
40	Sudan	14.2	4.7	2.8	2.7	25	13	47	39	40	54	5.6	25	5.6	4.1
41	Nepal	10.7	3.6	2.4	2.6	26	12	44	38	39	55	5.2	14	6.6	7.5
42	Gambia	0.5	0.2	3.1	3.7	32	18	50	42	33	46	5.4	26	5.0	6.0
43	Senegal	4.3	1.4	2.8	2.7	27	15	50	42	38	50	5.8	42	3.4	3.8
44	Yemen	7.8	2.8	2.3	3.8	28	14	53	47	36	51	7.4	34	6.3	7.2
45	Congo	1.3	0.5	2.7	2.9	23	15	45	44	42	51	6.1	59	4.3	5.3
46	Cameroon	6.7	2.3	2.6	2.8	24	12	44	40	40	57	5.5	45	6.9	5.2
47	Bolivia	3.5	1.1	2.4	2.2	22	10	46	35	43	60	4.6	61	3.2	4.1
48	Papua New Guinea	2.0	0.6	2.4	2.2	23	10	44	33	41	57	4.8	16	8.6	3.6
49	Kenya	15.5	5.3	3.6	3.5	22	12	53	44	45	55	6.0	28	7.7	7.1
50	Turkmenistan	1.9	0.6	2.8	2.4	15	7	44	30	56	66	3.8	45	2.8	2.1
51	Tajikistan	3.0	1.0	3.0	2.9	13	6	47	35	59	71	4.7	32	2.9	2.5
52	Namibia	0.7	0.2	2.6	2.7	22	10	44	36	43	60	5.1	37	4.6	6.0
53	Indonesia	77.9	21.9	2.3	1.8	23	8	44	24	42	64	2.8	35	4.6	4.9
54	Morocco	11.6	3.4	2.5	2.2	21	8	50	27	47	65	3.4	48	4.2	3.3
55	Mongolia	1.1	0.3	2.8	2.5	18	7	43	27	47	65	3.4	61	4.2	3.5
56	Zimbabwe	5.7	1.9	3.1	3.1	20	13	53	38	46	52	4.8	32	6.0	5.5
57	Iraq	10.2	3.4	3.3	3.0	20	6	49	37	49	67	5.5	75	5.0	3.9
58	Guatemala	5.4	1.8	2.8	2.9	19	7	49	38	46	66	5.1	42	3.4	3.5
59	South Africa	18.1	5.7	2.6	2.3	17	8	42	30	49	64	4.0	51	2.7	2.7
60	Libyan Arab Jamahiriya	2.8	1.0	4.2	3.8	19	8	49	41	47	64	6.2	86	10.4	5.2
61	Uzbekistan	10.5	3.2	2.9	2.4	13	6	43	30	60	70	3.7	41	3.9	2.5
62	Algeria	12.8	3.6	3.0	2.7	20	6	51	28	47	68	3.6	56	4.0	4.3
63	Brazil	62.1	17.8	2.4	1.9	13	7	43	24	55	67	2.8	78	4.3	3.0
64	Nicaragua	2.4	0.8	3.1	3.1	19	6	51	38	47	68	4.8	63	4.6	4.1
65	Peru	9.9	2.9	2.7	2.1	19	7	47	27	48	67	3.3	72	4.2	2.9
66	Kyrgyzstan	2.0	0.6	2.2	1.8	14	7	38	27	59	70	3.5	39	2.7	1.9
67	Philippines	30.2	9.3	2.7	2.2	15	6	46	29	53	67	3.8	54	3.9	4.7
68	Botswana	0.7	0.2	3.3	3.3	20	6	52	36	47	66	4.7	28	12.5	7.4
69	Egypt	27.9	8.1	2.2	2.4	21	8	45	28	46	65	3.7	45	2.7	2.6
70	Azerbaijan	2.8	0.8	2.0	1.4	10	6	40	21	64	71	2.4	56	2.5	1.7
71	Turkey	24.5	7.5	2.4	2.2	18	7	45	26	50	68	3.2	69	4.0	5.2
72	China	379.3	104.8	2.1	1.3	19	7	37	18	48	69	2.0	30	2.6	4.2
73	Kazakstan	6.0	1.6	1.5	0.9	12	7	34	19	60	70	2.4	60	2.4	1.6
74	Viet Nam	32.7	10.2	2.2	2.2	23	8	41	29	44	66	3.7	21	3.3	2.7
75	Dominican Rep.	3.2	1.0	2.7	2.1	16	5	50	26	52	70	2.9	65	5.1	3.8

		Population (millions) 1995		Population annual growth rate (%)		Crude death rate		Crude birth rate		Life expectancy		Total fertility rate 1995	% of population urbanized 1995	Average annual growth rate of urban population (%)	
		under 18	under 5	1965-80	1980-95	1960	1995	1960	1995	1960	1995			1965-80	1980-95
76	Albania	1.3	0.4	2.4	1.7	10	6	41	23	62	72	2.8	37	2.9	2.4
77	Ecuador	4.9	1.4	2.9	2.4	16	6	44	27	53	69	3.3	58	4.5	3.9
78	El Salvador	2.8	0.9	2.7	1.6	16	7	48	33	51	67	3.8	45	3.2	2.2
79	Iran, Islamic Rep. of	33.9	10.5	3.1	3.6	21	6	47	34	50	69	4.8	59	4.9	4.8
80	Lebanon	1.2	0.4	1.4	0.8	14	7	43	25	60	69	2.9	87	4.1	1.9
81	Honduras	2.9	0.9	3.1	3.1	19	6	52	35	47	69	4.6	44	5.1	4.6
82	Tunisia	3.7	1.0	2.1	2.2	19	6	47	24	49	69	3.0	57	3.9	2.9
83	Colombia	13.8	3.9	2.4	1.9	12	6	45	23	57	70	2.6	73	3.6	2.7
84	Syrian Arab Rep.	7.9	2.7	3.3	3.5	18	5	47	40	50	68	5.6	52	4.3	4.2
85	Moldova	1.4	0.3	1.2	0.7	13	11	26	15	62	68	2.1	52	3.7	2.4
86	Paraguay	2.3	0.7	2.8	3.1	9	5	43	31	64	71	4.1	53	3.8	4.6
87	Saudi Arabia	8.7	2.8	4.6	4.1	23	5	49	36	45	71	6.2	80	8.3	5.4
88	Mexico	39.6	11.8	2.9	2.2	13	5	45	26	58	71	3.0	75	4.2	3.1
89	Thailand	20.2	5.3	2.8	1.5	15	7	44	19	53	69	2.1	20	4.7	2.6
90	Armenia	1.3	0.4	2.2	1.1	9	6	35	19	68	73	2.5	69	3.3	1.4
91	TFYR Macedonia	0.6	0.2	1.3	1.2	12	7	32	15	61	72	2.0	60	3.2	2.0
92	Korea, Dem. Peo. Rep.	8.1	2.7	2.6	1.8	13	5	42	23	54	72	2.3	61	4.1	2.3
93	Russian Federation	37.5	7.8	0.6	0.4	8	13	22	10	69	68	1.5	76	1.8	1.0
94	Romania	5.8	1.2	1.0	0.2	9	11	20	11	66	70	1.5	55	2.8	1.0
95	Argentina	12.0	3.3	1.5	1.4	9	8	24	20	65	73	2.7	88	2.1	-1.8
96	Georgia	1.5	0.4	0.8	0.5	12	9	25	15	65	73	2.1	59	1.7	1.3
97	Latvia	0.6	0.1	0.7	0.1	10	13	16	11	70	69	1.6	73	1.7	0.5
98	Jordan	2.7	0.9	2.7	4.1	23	5	50	38	47	69	5.4	72	4.4	5.3
99	Oman	1.2	0.4	3.7	4.5	28	5	51	43	40	70	6.9	13	7.6	8.1
100	Ukraine	12.5	2.9	0.6	0.2	9	14	19	11	70	69	1.6	70	1.9	1.1
101	Venezuela	9.3	2.8	3.4	2.5	10	5	45	26	60	72	3.1	93	4.6	3.2
102	Yugoslavia	2.9	0.7	0.8	0.9	11	9	22	14	64	72	2.0	57	3.0	2.2
103	Mauritius	0.4	0.1	1.7	1.0	10	7	44	20	59	71	2.3	41	2.6	0.7
104	Estonia	0.4	0.1	0.9	0.2	11	13	16	11	69	69	1.6	73	1.8	0.5
105	Uruguay	0.9	0.3	0.5	0.6	10	10	22	17	68	73	2.3	90	0.9	1.0
106	Belarus	2.6	0.6	0.7	0.3	10	12	23	12	69	70	1.7	71	3.4	1.9
107	Panama	1.0	0.3	2.7	2.0	10	5	40	24	61	73	2.8	53	3.4	2.5
108	Bulgaria	2.0	0.4	0.5	-0.1	9	13	18	10	69	71	1.5	71	2.4	0.9
109	Lithuania	1.0	0.2	1.0	0.5	8	12	21	13	69	70	1.8	72	3.1	1.6
110	Sri Lanka	6.7	1.8	1.9	1.4	9	6	36	20	63	73	2.4	22	2.4	1.7
111	United Arab Emirates	0.7	0.2	13.0	4.2	19	3	46	22	53	74	4.1	84	15.6	5.3
112	Trinidad and Tobago	0.5	0.1	1.3	1.3	9	6	38	20	64	72	2.3	72	1.2	2.1
113	Bosnia and Herzegovina	0.9	0.2	0.9	-0.8	10	8	33	14	60	73	1.6	49	3.9	1.3
114	Poland	10.7	2.5	0.8	0.5	8	11	24	13	67	71	1.9	65	1.8	1.2
115	Costa Rica	1.4	0.4	2.9	2.7	10	4	47	25	62	77	3.0	50	3.7	3.6
116	Slovakia	1.5	0.4	0.9	0.5	8	11	22	14	70	71	1.9	59	3.1	1.3
117	Chile	4.9	1.5	1.8	1.6	13	6	38	21	57	74	2.5	84	2.6	1.9
118	Croatia	1.0	0.2	0.4	0.2	11	12	19	11	66	72	1.7	64	2.8	1.9
119	Hungary	2.3	0.6	0.4	-0.4	10	15	16	12	68	69	1.7	65	1.8	0.5
120	Kuwait	0.7	0.2	7.1	0.8	10	2	44	26	60	75	3.0	97	8.1	1.3
121	Jamaica	0.9	0.3	1.3	0.9	9	6	39	20	63	74	2.2	54	2.7	1.8
122	Malaysia	8.8	2.7	2.5	2.5	15	5	44	27	54	71	3.4	54	4.7	4.2
123	Portugal	2.3	0.6	0.4	0.0	11	11	24	12	63	75	1.6	36	1.8	1.3
124	Cuba	3.0	0.9	1.5	0.9	9	7	31	16	64	76	1.8	76	2.6	1.6
125	United States	68.6	20.4	1.1	1.0	9	9	23	15	70	76	2.1	76	1.2	1.2
126	Czech Rep.	2.5	0.7	0.4	0.0	11	13	15	13	70	71	1.8	65	2.1	0.2
127	Belgium	2.2	0.6	0.3	0.2	12	11	17	12	71	77	1.7	97	0.4	0.3
128	Greece	2.2	0.5	0.8	0.5	8	10	19	10	60	70	1.4	65	2.1	1.4
129	Spain	8.4	1.9	1.1	0.4	9	9	21	10	69	78	1.2	77	2.2	0.7
130	Korea, Rep. of	12.9	3.5	1.9	1.1	14	6	43	16	54	72	1.8	81	5.7	3.5
131	France	13.7	3.7	0.7	0.5	12	10	18	13	71	77	1.7	73	1.3	0.4
132	Israel	1.9	0.6	2.8	2.5	6	7	27	20	69	77	2.8	91	3.4	2.6
133	New Zealand	1.0	0.3	1.1	0.9	9	8	26	17	71	76	2.1	86	1.5	1.1
134	Slovenia	0.4	0.1	0.8	0.4	10	11	18	10	69	73	1.5	64	3.4	2.3
135	Australia	4.6	1.3	1.6	1.4	9	7	22	15	71	78	1.9	85	1.9	1.4
136	Italy	10.8	2.8	0.5	0.1	10	10	18	10	70	78	1.3	67	1.0	0.1
137	Netherlands	3.4	1.0	0.9	0.6	8	9	21	13	73	78	1.6	89	1.2	0.7
138	Norway	1.0	0.3	0.6	0.4	9	11	18	14	73	77	2.0	73	2.0	0.6
139	Canada	7.3	2.2	1.5	1.2	8	8	26	15	71	78	1.9	77	1.7	1.3
140	Austria	1.7	0.5	0.3	0.4	13	10	18	12	69	77	1.6	56	0.8	0.4
141	United Kingdom	13.5	3.9	0.2	0.2	12	11	17	13	71	77	1.8	90	0.4	0.3
142	Switzerland	1.5	0.4	0.5	0.9	10	9	18	13	72	78	1.6	61	1.0	1.3
143	Ireland	1.1	0.3	1.1	0.3	12	9	21	15	70	76	2.1	58	2.0	0.5
144	Germany	15.8	4.0	0.2	0.3	12	11	17	10	70	76	1.3	87	0.6	0.6
145	Denmark	1.1	0.3	0.5	0.1	9	12	17	12	72	76	1.7	85	1.0	0.2
146	Japan	25.3	6.2	1.1	0.5	8	8	18	10	68	80	1.5	78	1.9	0.6
147	Hong Kong*	1.4	0.3	2.1	1.0	7	6	35	10	67	79	1.2	95	2.5	1.3
148	Singapore	0.8	0.2	1.7	1.1	8	6	38	15	65	75	1.7	100	1.7	1.1
149	Finland	1.2	0.3	0.3	0.4	9	10	19	13	69	76	1.9	63	2.4	0.8
150	Sweden	2.0	0.6	0.5	0.4	10	11	15	14	74	79	2.1	83	1.0	0.4

Countries listed in descending order of their 1995 under-five mortality rates (Table 1).

Table 6: Economic indicators

		GNP per capita (US$) 1994	GNP per capita average annual growth rate (%)		Rate of inflation (%) 1985-94	% of population below absolute poverty level 1980-89		% of central government expenditure allocated to 1990-95			ODA inflow in millions US$ 1994	ODA inflow as a % of recipient GNP 1994	Debt service as a % of exports of goods and services	
			1965-80	1985-94		urban	rural	health	education	defence			1970	1994
1	Niger	230	-2.5	-2.1	0	..	35x	..	..	..	376	18	4	9
2	Angola	700x	..	-6.8	6	..	..	6x	15x	34x	451	6	..	3
3	Sierra Leone	160	0.7	-0.4	68	..	65x	10	13	10	276	39	11	16
4	Mozambique	90	..	3.8	53	50	67	5x	10x	35x	1231	88	..	19
5	Afghanistan	280x	0.6	..	..	18x	36x	..	..	..	228	4	..	..
6	Guinea-Bissau	240	-2.7	2.2	66	..	..	1x	3x	4x	177	70	..	11
7	Guinea	520	1.3	1.3	19	..	..	3x	11x	29x	360	11	..	13
8	Malawi	170	3.2	-0.7	19	25	85	7x	12x	5x	470	26	8	16
9	Liberia	450x	0.5	..	..	..	23x	5x	11x	9x	63	5	8	..
10	Somalia	120x	-0.1	-2.3	75	40x	70x	1x	2x	38x	538	49	2	7
11	Mali	250	2.1x	1.0	3	27x	48x	2x	9x	8x	442	17	1	25
12	Zambia	350	-1.2	-1.4	92	25	..	14	15	..	719	22	6	26
13	Eritrea	100x	..	..	..	..	..	..	..	..	158	46	..	..
14	Ethiopia	100	0.4	-0.6	6	60	65	3	11	40	1070	20	11	11
15	Mauritania	480	-0.1	0.2	7	..	..	4x	23x	..	269	25	3	21
16	Nigeria	280	4.2	1.2	30	..	..	1x	3x	3x	190	1	4	19
17	Bhutan	400	..	4.4	8	..	..	8	11	..	77	12	..	7
18	Uganda	190	-2.2	2.3	75	..	..	2x	15x	26x	753	19	3	36
19	Zaire	220x	-1.3	-1.0	..	..	80x	1	1	3	245	3	5	6
20	Burundi	160	2.4	-0.7	5	55x	85x	4x	16x	16x	310	31	4	21
21	Cambodia	200x	..	..	..	..	..	..	..	..	337	17	..	0
22	Central African Rep.	370	0.8	-2.7	4	..	91	..	..	..	166	14	5	9
23	Burkina Faso	300	1.7	-0.1	2	..	..	7	17	14	435	14	4	7
24	Madagascar	200	-0.4	-1.7	16	50x	50x	7	17	8	289	10	32	6
25	Tanzania , U. Rep. of	140	0.8	0.8	23	..	..	6x	8x	16x	968	24	1	18
26	Lesotho	720	6.8	0.6	14	50x	55x	12	22	7	117	8	1	4
27	Chad	180	-1.9	0.7	2	30x	56x	8x	8x	..	215	19	4	7
28	Côte d'Ivoire	610	2.8	-4.6	0	30	26	4x	21x	4x	1594	19	7	21
29	Myanmar	220x	1.6	..	25	40x	40x	5	15	39	162	2	18	15
30	Gabon	3880	5.6	-3.7	3	..	..	..	..	..	182	4	6	8
31	Benin	370	-0.3	-0.8	3	..	..	6x	31x	17x	257	13	2	10
32	Rwanda	80	1.6	-6.6	4	30	90x	5x	26x	..	713	115	1	11
33	Pakistan	430	1.8	1.3	9	32x	29x	1	2	31	1606	3	22	29
34	Lao Peo. Dem. Rep.	320	..	2.1	24	..	..	..	..	..	218	14	..	8
35	Ghana	410	-0.8	1.4	28	59	37	7	22	5	546	8	5	16
36	Togo	320	1.7	-2.7	4	42x	..	5x	20x	11x	126	10	3	4
37	Haiti	230	0.9	-5.0	13	65	80	..	..	..	601	37	5	0
38	Bangladesh	220	-0.3	2.0	7	86x	86x	5x	11x	10x	1757	7	0	14
39	India	320	1.5	2.9	10	29	33	2	2	15	2324	1	21	20
40	Sudan	480x	0.8	-0.2	55	..	85x	..	..	..	412	3	11	0
41	Nepal	200	..	2.3	12	55x	61x	5	11	6	448	10	3	12
42	Gambia	330	..	0.5	11	..	..	7	12	4	70	20	1	16
43	Senegal	600	-0.5	-0.7	3	..	..	..	..	..	644	13	4	11
44	Yemen	280	..	..	..	..	..	5	21	30	172	4	..	4
45	Congo	620	2.7	-2.9	0	..	..	..	..	..	362	23	11	49
46	Cameroon	680	2.4	-6.9	1	15x	40x	5	18	9	731	8	3	13
47	Bolivia	770	1.7	1.7	20	..	..	7	19	8	578	10	11	24
48	Papua New Guinea	1240	..	2.2	4	10x	75x	9	18	3	326	6	1	10
49	Kenya	250	3.1	0.0	12	10x	55x	5	19	6	676	10	6	27
50	Turkmenistan	1230x	..	-1.5	46	..	..	..	..	..	19	0	..	4
51	Tajikistan	360	..	-11.4	104	..	..	..	..	..	49	2	..	..
52	Namibia	1970	..	3.3	11	..	..	10	22	7	138	5	..	..
53	Indonesia	880	5.2	6.0	9	20	16	3	10	6	1642	1	7	19
54	Morocco	1140	2.7	1.2	5	28x	45x	3	18	14	631	2	8	30
55	Mongolia	300	..	-3.2	46	..	..	4	7	12	184	26	..	9
56	Zimbabwe	500	1.7	-0.5	20	..	..	8x	24x	17x	561	10	2	20
57	Iraq	1036x	..	..	..	..	..	..	..	..	259	1	..	..
58	Guatemala	1200	3.0	0.9	20	17	51	11	19	15	224	2	7	9
59	South Africa	3040	3.2	-1.3	14	..	..	..	..	..	294	0	..	..
60	Libyan Arab Jamahiriya	5310x	0.0	..	..	..	..	..	..	..	7	0	..	..
61	Uzbekistan	960	..	-2.3	93	..	..	..	..	..	23	0	..	3
62	Algeria	1650	4.2	-2.5	22	20x	..	..	..	..	420	1	3	53
63	Brazil	2970	6.3	-0.4	913	9	34	5	4	3	336	0	12	17
64	Nicaragua	340	-0.7	-6.1	1315	21x	19x	13	16	6	600	41	11	36
65	Peru	2110	0.8	-2.0	495	46	83	5	16	11	416	1	12	16
66	Kyrgyzstan	630	..	-5.0	101	..	..	..	..	..	154	5	..	4
67	Philippines	950	3.2	1.7	10	52	64	3	16	11	1057	2	8	14
68	Botswana	2800	9.9	6.6	12	40	55	5	20	12	89	2	1	4
69	Egypt	720	2.8	1.3	16	34	34	2	12	9	2695	6	26	12
70	Azerbaijan	500	..	-12.2	123	..	..	..	..	..	70	2	..	..
71	Turkey	2500	3.6	1.4	66	..	..	3	14	10	163	0	16	23
72	China	530	4.1	7.8	10	..	13	0	3	19	3232	1	0x	8
73	Kazakhstan	1160	..	-6.5	150	..	..	..	..	..	48	0	..	2
74	Viet Nam	200	..	..	103	..	..	..	..	..	897	6	..	5
75	Dominican Rep.	1330	3.8	2.2	29	45x	43x	11	10	5	68	1	4	18

		GNP per capita (US$) 1994	GNP per capita average annual growth rate (%)		Rate of inflation (%) 1985-94	% of population below absolute poverty level 1980-89		% of central government expenditure allocated to 1990-95			ODA inflow in millions US$ 1994	ODA inflow as a % of recipient GNP 1994	Debt service as a % of exports of goods and services	
			1965-80	1985-94		urban	rural	health	education	defence			1970	1994
76	Albania	380	..	-6.0	33						164	13		2
77	Ecuador	1280	5.4	0.9	48	40	65	11	18	13	217	2	9	19
78	El Salvador	1360	1.5	2.2	16	20	32	8	13	8	316	4	4	14
79	Iran, Islamic Rep. of	1033x	2.9	-1.0	22			9	16	7	131	0		19
80	Lebanon	2150x	..	..	..						235	4		8
81	Honduras	600	1.1	0.5	12	31	70	10x	19x	7x	298	9	3	31
82	Tunisia	1790	4.7	2.1	6	20x	15x	7	18	5	105	1	18	17
83	Colombia	1670	3.7	2.4	25	32	70	5	19	9	127	0	12	26
84	Syrian Arab Rep.	1160x	5.1	-2.1	22			2	10	31	745	5	11	3
85	Moldova	870												1
86	Paraguay	1580	4.1	1.0	26	19x	50x	7	22	11	103	1	12	9
87	Saudi Arabia	7050	4.0x	-1.7	3			6x	14x	36x	20	0		
88	Mexico	4180	3.6	0.9	40			2	14	2	431	0	24	21
89	Thailand	2410	4.4	8.6	5	10	25	8	21	17	578	0	3	5
90	Armenia	680	..	-13.0	134						142	6		2
91	TFYR Macedonia	820	..	..	..									11
92	Korea, Dem. Peo. Rep.	970x	..	..	..			1	..	16	6	0		6
93	Russian Federation	2650	..	-4.1	124			1	3	16				6
94	Romania	1270	..	-4.5	64			8	10	7			0x	4
95	Argentina	8110	1.7	2.0	317			3	9	7	225	0	22	22
96	Georgia	580x	..	-18.6	234						105	3		3
97	Latvia	2320	..	-6.0	70			6	15	3				2
98	Jordan	1440	5.8	-5.6	7	14x	17x	7	16	21	370	5	4	11
99	Oman	5140	9.0	0.5	0			6	13	37	95	1		10
100	Ukraine	1910	..	-8.0	160									2
101	Venezuela	2760	2.3	0.7	37			10x	20x	6x	31	0	3	12
102	Yugoslavia	a									1716			
103	Mauritius	3150	3.7	5.8	9	12x	12x	9	17	2	14	0	3	5
104	Estonia	2820	..	-6.1	78			17	9	3				1
105	Uruguay	4660	2.5	2.9	74	22	..	6	7	7	86	1	22	12
106	Belarus	2160	..	-1.9	138			3	18	4				4
107	Panama	2580	2.8	-1.2	2	21x	30x	20	20	5	40	1	8	5
108	Bulgaria	1250	..	-2.7	42			3	3	6				12
109	Lithuania	1350	..	-8.0	102			5	7	2				2
110	Sri Lanka	640	2.8	2.9	11			6	11	12	595	5	11	9
111	United Arab Emirates	21430x	..	0.4	..			7	17	37	-7	0		
112	Trinidad and Tobago	3740	3.1	-2.3	7		39x				21	0	5	27
113	Bosnia and Herzegovina	b												
114	Poland	2410	..	0.8	102									13
115	Costa Rica	2400	3.3	2.8	18	8	20	21	23	..	76	1	10	11
116	Slovakia	2250	..	-3.0	10			12	14	9	157	0		7
117	Chile	3520	0.0	6.5	19	12	20	12	14	9	157	0	19	8
118	Croatia	2560						14	7	19				2
119	Hungary	3840	5.1	-1.2	20			8	3	4				43
120	Kuwait	19420	0.6x	1.1	..			6	11	22	6	0		
121	Jamaica	1540	-0.1	3.9	28	..	80	7x	11x	8x	114	3	3	18
122	Malaysia	3480	4.7	5.6	3	13	38	6	22	13	68	0	4	6
123	Portugal	9320	4.6	4.0	12			9x	11x	6x			7	16
124	Cuba	1170x	..	..				23x	10x	..	47	0		
125	United States	25880	1.8	1.3	3			18	2	18 ..				
126	Czech Rep.	3200	..	-2.1	12			17	11	6				6
127	Belgium	22870	3.6	2.3	3			2x	12x	5x				
128	Greece	7700	4.8	1.3	10			7	9	9	44x	0x	9	
129	Spain	13440	4.1	2.8	7			6	4	4				
130	Korea, Rep. of	8260	7.3	7.8	7	18x	11x	1	20	18	-114	0	20	4
131	France	23420	3.7	1.6	3			16	7	6				
132	Israel	14530	3.7	2.3	18			6	14	19	1237	2	3	
133	New Zealand	13350	1.7	0.7	5			16	15	4				
134	Slovenia	7040												2
135	Australia	18000	2.2	1.2	4			13	8	8				
136	Italy	19300	3.2	1.8	6			11x	8x	4x				
137	Netherlands	22010	2.7	1.9	2			14	10	4				
138	Norway	26390	3.6	1.4	3			10	10	7				
139	Canada	19510	3.3	0.3	3			6	3	7				
140	Austria	24630	4.0	2.0	3			13	10	2				
141	United Kingdom	18340	2.0	1.3	5			14	3	10				
142	Switzerland	37930	1.5	0.5	4			13x	3x	10x				
143	Ireland	13530	2.8	5.0	2			14	13	3				
144	Germany	25580	3.0x	1.9	3			17	1	7				
145	Denmark	27970	2.2	1.3	3			1	11	5				
146	Japan	34630	5.1	3.2	1			2	6	4				
147	Hong Kong*	21650	6.2	5.3	9			8x	17x	..	27	0		
148	Singapore	22500	8.3	6.1	4			6	25	25	17	0	1	
149	Finland	18850	3.6	-0.3	4			3	11	4				
150	Sweden	23530	2.0	-0.1	6			0	5	6				

Countries listed in descending order of their 1995 under-five mortality rates (table 1).
a: Range US$726 to US$2895. b: Range US$725 or less.

Table 7: Women

		Life expectancy females as a % of males 1995	Adult literacy rate females as a % of males 1995	Enrolment ratios females as a % of males 1990-94		Contraceptive prevalence (%) 1990-96	% of pregnant women immunized against tetanus 1992-95	% of births attended by trained health personnel 1990-96	Maternal mortality rate 1990
				primary school	secondary school				
1	Niger	107	33	60	44	4	57	15	1200
2	Angola	107	52x	92	..	1x	14	15x	1500
3	Sierra Leone	108	40	70	55	4x	61	25x	1800
4	Mozambique	107	40	74	67	4x	61	25x	1500
5	Afghanistan	102	32	35	36	2x	3	9x	1700
6	Guinea-Bissau	107	63	55x	44x	1x	53	27x	910
7	Guinea	102	44	49	35	2	56	31	1600
8	Malawi	103	58	92	50	13	77	55	560
9	Liberia	105	41	55x	39x	6x	77	58x	560
10	Somalia	107	39x	53x	56x	1x	11	2x	1600
11	Mali	107	59	63	50	7	19	24	1200
12	Zambia	103	83	92x	56x	15	44	51	940
13	Eritrea	106	..	79	76	8	19	21	1400
14	Ethiopia	107	54	70	92	4	22	14x	1400
15	Mauritania	106	52	82	58	4	28	40	930
16	Nigeria	106	70	78	84	6	21	31	1000
17	Bhutan	107	50	61x	29x	19	70	15	1600
18	Uganda	105	68	80	57	15	76	38	1200
19	Zaire	106	78	74	45	8	33	..	870
20	Burundi	107	47	82	63	9x	30	19x	1300
21	Cambodia	105	46x	..	..	..	36	47x	900
22	Central African Rep.	110	75	63x	35x	15	50	46	700
23	Burkina Faso	107	30	64	55	8	39	42	930
24	Madagascar	105	83x	96	100	17	33	57	490
25	Tanzania , U. Rep. of	106	72	97	83	20	71	53	770
26	Lesotho	108	77	117	141	23	12	40x	610
27	Chad	107	56	48	15	1x	50	15	1500
28	Côte d'Ivoire	105	60	73	52	11	22	45	810
29	Myanmar	106	88	97	100	17	83	57x	580
30	Gabon	106	72	..	..	..	29	80x	500
31	Benin	107	53	50	41	9x	77	45x	990
32	Rwanda	106	74	97	82	21	88	26	1300
33	Pakistan	103	48	53	46	12	36	19	340
34	Lao Peo. Dem. Rep.	106	64	75	61	19	35	..	650
35	Ghana	107	71	84	64	20	64	44	740
36	Togo	107	55	66	35	12x	43	54x	640
37	Haiti	106	88	93	95	18	49	21	1000
38	Bangladesh	100	53	87	52	45	78	14	850
39	India	100	58	81	64	41	79	34	570
40	Sudan	105	60	76	79	8	65	69	660
41	Nepal	99	34	67	50	23	11	7	1500
42	Gambia	107	47	71	52	12	93	44	1100
43	Senegal	104	53	75	52	7	39	46	1200
44	Yemen	101	49x	39	21	7	3	16	1400
45	Congo	109	81	..	..	..	75	..	890
46	Cameroon	105	69	85	72	16	12	64	550
47	Bolivia	106	84	91	85	45	65	47	650
48	Papua New Guinea	103	78	84	67	4x	31	20x	930
49	Kenya	105	81	99	82	33	72	45	650
50	Turkmenistan	111	98x	..	..	..	..	..	55
51	Tajikistan	108	98x	97	103	..	..	..	130
52	Namibia	104	..	103	124	29	72	68	370
53	Indonesia	106	87	97	81	55	74	36	650
54	Morocco	106	54	71	73	50	37	40	610
55	Mongolia	104	87	105	114x	..	..	99x	65
56	Zimbabwe	105	89	93	78	48	46	69	570
57	Iraq	105	63	85	64	18x	72	54x	310
58	Guatemala	108	78	88	92	31	55	35	200
59	South Africa	110	100	99	118	50x	26	82	230
60	Libyan Arab Jamahiriya	106	72	100	100	..	45	76x	220
61	Uzbekistan	109	98x	99	96	..	..	..	55
62	Algeria	104	66	86	83	57	52	77	160
63	Brazil	107	100	96x	116x	66x	70	81	220
64	Nicaragua	106	103	104	113	49	49	61	160
65	Peru	106	87	96x	91x	59	21	52	280
66	Kyrgyzstan	111	98x	..	..	..	..	..	110
67	Philippines	106	99	99x	102x	40	48	53	280
68	Botswana	106	74	106	112	33x	56	78x	250
69	Egypt	104	61	85	85	48	64	46	170
70	Azerbaijan	112	97x	96	99	..	..	..	22
71	Turkey	106	78	92	65	63	38	76	180
72	China	105	81	97	85	83	11	84	95
73	Kazakstan	113	97x	100	102	59	..	99	80
74	Viet Nam	107	94	94x	93x	65	82	95x	160
75	Dominican Rep.	106	100	104	143	56	52	92	110

		Life expectancy females as a % of males 1995	Adult literacy rate females as a % of males 1995	Enrolment ratios females as a % of males 1990-94		Contraceptive prevalence (%) 1990-96	% of pregnant women immunized against tetanus 1992-95	% of births attended by trained health personnel 1990-96	Maternal mortality rate 1990
				primary school	secondary school				
76	Albania	108	..	102	86	..	..	99x	65
77	Ecuador	108	96	98	104	57	21	64	150
78	El Salvador	108	95	101	111	53	80	87	300
79	Iran, Islamic Rep. of	102	76	93	78	73	82	77	120
80	Lebanon	106	95	97	107	55x	..	45x	300
81	Honduras	107	100	101	128	47	48	88	220
82	Tunisia	103	70	92	89	60	49	69x	170
83	Colombia	109	100	102	119	72	57	85	100
84	Syrian Arab Rep.	106	65	89	81	36	76	67	180
85	Moldova	113	95x	99	107	..	..	..	60
86	Paraguay	105	97	96	106	48	66	66	160
87	Saudi Arabia	105	69	94	80	..	62	82x	130
88	Mexico	109	95	96	102	53x	42	77	110
89	Thailand	109	96	99	97	74	93	71x	200
90	Armenia	109	99x	107	113	..	..	..	50
91	TFYR Macedonia	109	..	99	104	..	91	..	..
92	Korea, Dem. Peo. Rep.	109	..	94x	..	..	95	100x	70
93	Russian Federation	119	98x	99	108	..	..	..	75
94	Romania	110	96x	99	99	57	..	100x	130
95	Argentina	110	100	99	107	74x	..	97	100
96	Georgia	112	99x	..	..	..	..	..	33
97	Latvia	118	99x	99	107	..	..	..	40
98	Jordan	106	85	101	104	35	59	87	150
99	Oman	106	65	94	89	9x	95	87x	190
100	Ukraine	115	98x	100	146	..	..	100x	50
101	Venezuela	108	98	102	141	49x	18	69x	120
102	Yugoslavia	107	91x	101	102	..	..	..	..
103	Mauritius	110	91	99	103	75	78	97	120
104	Estonia	117	100x	99	110	70	..	..	41
105	Uruguay	109	101	99	102x	..	13	96x	85
106	Belarus	116	98x	99	108	50	..	100x	37
107	Panama	106	99	96	108	58x	24	86	55
108	Bulgaria	110	98x	97	106	76x	..	100x	27
109	Lithuania	117	99x	95	104	..	..	..	36
110	Sri Lanka	106	94	99	110	66	81	94	140
111	United Arab Emirates	103	101	96	112	..	..	96x	26
112	Trinidad and Tobago	107	98	100	105	53x	19	98x	90
113	Bosnia and Herzegovina	108	..	..	..	..	..	..	..
114	Poland	113	99x	99	106	75x	..	99x	19
115	Costa Rica	106	100	99	109	75	90	93x	60
116	Slovakia	113	..	100	103	74	..	..	..
117	Chile	110	100	99	108	43x	..	98x	65
118	Croatia	113	96x	100	108	..	93	..	..
119	Hungary	114	99x	100	104	73x	..	99x	30
120	Kuwait	105	91	100	100	35x	21	99x	29
121	Jamaica	106	110	99	113	62	82	82x	120
122	Malaysia	106	88	100	109	48x	79	94	80
123	Portugal	110	91x	97	117	66x	..	90x	15
124	Cuba	105	99	100	111	70x	61	90x	95
125	United States	109	..	99	99	74x	..	99x	12
126	Czech Rep.	110	..	101	104	69	..	..	15
127	Belgium	109	..	101	101	79	..	100x	10
128	Greece	107	95x	101	98	..	..	97x	10
129	Spain	108	96x	101	112	59x	..	96x	7
130	Korea, Rep. of	111	98	102	99	79	..	98	130
131	France	110	..	98	103	75	..	99	15
132	Israel	105	94x	101	108	..	..	99x	7
133	New Zealand	108	..	99	101	70x	..	99x	25
134	Slovenia	114	..	100	102	..	..	..	13
135	Australia	108	..	99	104	76x	..	100	9
136	Italy	109	98x	101	101	78x	..	..	12
137	Netherlands	108	..	103	95	80	..	100x	12
138	Norway	109	..	100	97	76x	..	100x	6
139	Canada	109	..	98	99	73x	..	99x	6
140	Austria	108	..	100	95	71x	..	100	10
141	United Kingdom	107	..	101	103	82	..	100x	9
142	Switzerland	109	..	102	96	71x	..	99x	6
143	Ireland	108	..	100	109	..	..	..	10
144	Germany	109	..	101	99	75	..	99	22
145	Denmark	108	..	101	103	78x	..	100x	9
146	Japan	108	..	100	102	59	..	100x	18
147	Hong Kong*	108	92	99x	106x	81x	..	100x	7
148	Singapore	107	90	98x	103x	74x	..	100x	10
149	Finland	111	..	100	118	80x	..	100	11
150	Sweden	108	..	100	101	78x	..	100x	7

Countries listed in descending order of their 1995 under-five mortality rates (table 1).

Table 8: Basic indicators on less populous countries

		Under-5 mortality rate		Infant mortality rate (under 1)		Total population (thousands) 1995	Annual no. of births (thousands) 1995	Annual no. of under-5 deaths (thousands) 1995	GNP per capita (US$) 1994	Life expectancy at birth (years) 1995	Total adult literacy rate 1995	% of age group enrolled in primary school (gross) 1990-93	% of children immunized against measles 1992-95
		1960	1995	1960	1995								
1	Equatorial Guinea	316	175	188	113	400	17.0	3.0	430	49	79	149x	61
2	Djibouti	289	158	186	113	577	22.0	3.5	780x	49	46	36	42
3	Comoros	248	124	165	85	653	31.0	3.8	510	57	57	75	59
4	Swaziland	233	107	157	74	855	32.0	3.4	1100	59	77	120	93
5	Marshall Islands	..	92	..	63	54	1.4x	0.1	1680	..	91x	95	59
6	Sao Tome/Principe	..	81	..	63	133	4.6	0.4	250	69	57x	..	47
7	Kiribati	..	77	..	57	79	2.2	0.2	740	60	93x	91	96
8	Maldives	258	77	158	55	254	10.0	0.8	950	63	93	134	62
9	Cape Verde	164	73	110	54	392	14.0	1.0	930	66	72	123	66
10	Guyana	126	59	100	44	835	20.0	1.2	530	66	98	112x	84
11	Vanuatu	225	58	141	44	169	6.0	0.4	1150	66	64x	106	53
12	Tuvalu	..	56	..	40	10	..	..	650x	..	99x	101	94
13	Samoa	210	54	134	43	171	6.0	0.3	1000	69	98x	100	98
14	Belize	104	40	74	32	215	7.0	0.3	2530	74	70x	109	83
15	Saint Kitts/Nevis	..	40	..	32	41	0.8	0.0	4760	69	90x	..	99
16	Palau	..	35	..	25	17	0.3x	0.0	790x	..	98x	103	100
17	Grenada	..	33	..	26	92	2.1	0.1	2630	72	98x	88x	84
18	Suriname	96	32	70	26	423	10.0	0.3	860	71	93	127x	69
19	Solomon Islands	185	31	120	25	378	14.0	0.4	810	71	62x	94	68
20	Turks/Caicos Islands	..	31	..	25	14	0.2x	0.0	780x	..	98x	..	100
21	Bahamas	68	28	51	23	276	5.0	0.1	11800	74	98	97	88
22	British Virgin Islands	..	28	..	24	19	0.2x	0.0	8500x	..	98x	..	100
23	Cook Islands	..	28	..	26	19	0.4x	0.0	1550x	..	99x	98	96
24	Micronesia, Fed. States of	..	28	..	22	124	4.1	0.1	1890	64	81x	100	90
25	Fiji	97	25	71	21	784	18.0	0.5	2250	72	92	128	94
26	Tonga	..	24	..	20	98	2.6	0.1	1590	69	99x	98x	94
27	Qatar	239	23	145	18	551	11.0	0.3	12820	71	79	90	86
28	Saint Vincent/Grenadines	..	23	..	19	112	2.3	0.1	2140	72	82x	95x	100
29	Antigua/Barbuda	..	22	..	18	66	1.0	0.0	6770	75	95x	100x	94
30	Saint Lucia	..	22	..	18	142	3.6	0.1	3130	71	82x	95x	94
31	Dominica	..	21	..	17	71	1.5	0.0	2800	73	94x	..	92
32	Bahrain	203	20	130	17	564	15.0	0.3	7460	72	85	111	89
33	Seychelles	..	20	..	16	73	1.6	0.0	6680	72	88x	102x	99
34	Montserrat	..	14	..	11	11	0.2	0.0	3330x	73	97x	100x	100
35	Malta	42	12	37	10	366	5.0	0.1	7970x	77	86x	108	90
36	Barbados	90	10	74	9	262	4.0	0.0	6560	76	97	90	92
37	Cyprus	36	10	30	9	742	13.0	0.1	10260	77	94x	101	83
38	Brunei Darussalam	87	10	63	8	285	6.0	0.1	14240	75	88	107	100
39	Luxembourg	41	9	33	8	406	5.0	0.1	39600	76	..	91	80
40	Iceland	22	5	17	5	269	5.0	0.0	24630	79	..	100	98

Measuring human development

An introduction to table 9

If development in the 1990s is to assume a more human face then there arises a corresponding need for a means of measuring human as well as economic progress. From UNICEF's point of view, in particular, there is a need for an agreed method of measuring the level of child well-being and its rate of change.

The under-five mortality rate (U5MR) is used in table 9 (next page) as the principal indicator of such progress.

The U5MR has several advantages. First, it measures an end result of the development process rather than an 'input' such as school enrolment level, per capita calorie availability, or the number of doctors per thousand population — all of which are means to an end.

Second, the U5MR is known to be the result of a wide variety of inputs: the nutritional health and the health knowledge of mothers; the level of immunization and ORT use; the availability of maternal and child health services (including prenatal care); income and food availability in the family; the availability of clean water and safe sanitation; and the overall safety of the child's environment.

Third, the U5MR is less susceptible than, say, per capita GNP to the fallacy of the average. This is because the natural scale does not allow the children of the rich to be one thousand times as likely to survive, even if the man-made scale does permit them to have one thousand times as much income. In other words, it is much more difficult for a wealthy minority to affect a nation's U5MR, and it therefore presents a more accurate, if far from perfect, picture of the health status of the majority of children (and of society as a whole).

For these reasons, the U5MR is chosen by UNICEF as its single most important indicator of the state of a nation's children. That is why the statistical annex lists the nations of the world not in ascending order of their per capita GNP but in descending order of their under-five mortality rates.

The speed of progress in reducing the U5MR can be measured by calculating its average annual reduction rate (AARR). Unlike the comparison of absolute changes, the AARR reflects the fact that the lower limits to U5MR are approached only with increasing difficulty. As lower levels of under-five mortality are reached, for example, the same absolute reduction obviously represents a greater percentage of reduction. The AARR therefore shows a higher rate of progress for, say, a 10-point reduction if that reduction happens at a lower level of under-five mortality. (A fall in U5MR of 10 points from 100 to 90 represents a reduction of 10 per cent, whereas the same 10-point fall from 20 to 10 represents a reduction of 50 per cent).

When used in conjunction with GNP growth rates, the U5MR and its reduction rate can therefore give a picture of the progress being made by any country or region, and over any period of time, towards the satisfaction of some of the most essential of human needs.

As table 9 shows, there is no fixed relationship between the annual reduction rate of the U5MR and the annual rate of growth in per capita GNP. Such comparisons help to throw the emphasis on to the policies, priorities, and other factors which determine the ratio between economic and social progress.

Finally, the table gives the total fertility rate for each country and its average annual rate of reduction. It will be seen that many of the nations that have achieved significant reductions in their U5MR have also achieved significant reductions in fertility.

Table 9: The rate of progress

		Under-5 mortality rate			average annual rate of reduction (%)			GNP per capita average annual growth rate (%)		Total fertility rate			average annual rate of reduction (%)	
		1960	1980	1995	1960-80	1980-95	required* 1995-2000	1965-80	1985-94	1960	1980	1995	1960-80	1980-95
1	Niger	320	320	320	0.0	0.0	30.4	-2.5	-2.1	7.3	8.1	7.3	-0.5	0.7
2	Angola	345	261	292	1.4	-0.7	28.6	..	-6.8	6.4	6.9	6.9	-0.4	0.0
3	Sierra Leone	385	301	284	1.2	0.4	28.0	0.7	-0.4	6.2	6.5	6.3	-0.2	0.2
4	Mozambique	331	269	275	1.0	-0.1	27.4	..	3.8	6.3	6.5	6.3	-0.2	0.2
5	Afghanistan	360	280	257	1.3	0.6	26.0	0.6	..	6.9	7.1	6.6	-0.1	0.5
6	Guinea-Bissau	336	290	227	0.7	1.6	23.5	-2.7	2.2	5.1	5.7	5.6	-0.6	0.1
7	Guinea	337	276	219	1.0	1.5	22.8	1.3	1.3	7.0	7.0	6.8	0.0	0.2
8	Malawi	365	290	219	1.1	1.9	22.8	3.2	-0.7	6.9	7.6	6.9	-0.5	0.6
9	Liberia	288	235	216	1.0	0.6	22.5	0.5	..	6.6	6.8	6.6	-0.1	0.2
10	Somalia	294	246	211	0.9	1.0	22.1	-0.1	-2.3	7.0	7.0	6.8	0.0	0.2
11	Mali	400	310	210	1.3	2.6	22.0	2.1x	1.0	7.1	7.1	6.9	0.0	0.2
12	Zambia	220	160	203	1.6	-1.6	21.3	-1.2	-1.4	6.6	7.1	5.7	-0.4	1.5
13	Eritrea	294	260	195	0.6	1.9	20.5	..	..	6.6	6.1	5.6	0.4	0.6
14	Ethiopia	294	260	195	0.6	1.9	20.5	0.4	-0.6	6.9	6.9	6.8	0.0	0.1
15	Mauritania	321	249	195	1.3	1.6	20.5	-0.1	0.2	6.5	6.3	5.2	0.2	1.3
16	Nigeria	204	196	191	0.2	0.2	20.1	4.2	1.2	6.5	6.5	6.2	0.0	0.3
17	Bhutan	324	249	189	1.3	1.8	19.9	..	4.4	6.0	5.9	5.7	0.1	0.2
18	Uganda	218	181	185	0.9	-0.2	19.4	-2.2	2.3	6.9	7.0	7.0	-0.1	0.0
19	Zaire	286	204	185	1.7	0.6	19.4	-1.3	-1.0	6.0	6.6	6.5	-0.5	0.1
20	Burundi	255	193	176	1.4	0.6	18.4	2.4	-0.7	6.8	6.8	6.5	0.0	0.3
21	Cambodia	217	330	174	-2.1	4.3	18.2	..	..	6.3	4.6	5.1	1.6	-0.7
22	Central African Rep.	294	202	165	1.9	1.4	17.1	0.8	-2.7	5.6	5.8	5.5	-0.2	0.4
23	Burkina Faso	318	246	164	1.3	2.7	17.0	1.7	-0.1	6.4	6.5	6.3	-0.1	0.2
24	Madagascar	364	216	164	2.6	1.8	17.0	-0.4	-1.7	6.6	6.6	5.9	0.0	0.7
25	Tanzania , U. Rep. of	249	180	160	1.6	0.8	16.5	0.8	0.8	6.8	6.8	5.7	0.0	1.2
26	Lesotho	204	173	154	0.8	0.8	15.8	6.8	0.6	5.8	5.7	5.0	0.1	0.9
27	Chad	325	206	152	2.3	2.0	15.5	-1.9	0.7	6.0	5.9	5.7	0.1	0.2
28	Côte d'Ivoire	300	170	150	2.8	0.8	15.2	2.8	-4.6	7.2	7.4	7.1	-0.1	0.3
29	Myanmar	237	146	150	2.4	-0.2	15.2	1.6	..	6.0	5.1	4.0	0.8	1.6
30	Gabon	287	194	148	2.0	1.8	15.0	5.6	-3.7	4.1	4.4	5.5	-0.4	-1.5
31	Benin	310	176	142	2.8	1.4	14.1	-0.3	-0.8	6.9	7.1	6.9	-0.1	0.2
32	Rwanda	191	222	139	-0.8	3.1	13.7	1.6	-6.6	7.5	8.3	6.3	-0.5	1.8
33	Pakistan	221	151	137	1.9	0.6	13.4	1.8	1.3	6.9	7.0	5.9	-0.1	1.1
34	Lao Peo. Dem. Rep.	233	190	134	1.0	2.3	13.0	..	2.1	6.2	6.7	6.4	-0.4	0.3
35	Ghana	213	155	130	1.6	1.2	12.4	-0.8	1.4	6.9	6.5	5.7	0.3	0.9
36	Togo	264	175	128	2.0	2.1	12.1	1.7	-2.7	6.6	6.6	6.3	0.0	0.3
37	Haiti	260	195	124	1.4	3.0	11.4	0.9	-5.0	6.3	5.3	4.7	0.9	0.8
38	Bangladesh	247	211	115	0.8	4.0	9.9	-0.3	2.0	6.7	6.4	4.1	0.2	3.0
39	India	236	177	115	1.4	2.9	9.9	1.5	2.9	5.9	4.7	3.6	1.1	1.8
40	Sudan	292	200	115	1.9	3.7	9.9	0.8	-0.2	6.7	6.5	5.6	0.2	1.0
41	Nepal	290	180	114	2.4	3.0	9.8	..	2.3	5.7	6.4	5.2	-0.6	1.4
42	Gambia	375	250	110	2.0	5.5	9.0	..	0.5	6.4	6.5	5.4	-0.1	1.2
43	Senegal	303	221	110	1.6	4.6	9.0	-0.5	-0.7	7.0	6.9	5.8	0.1	1.2
44	Yemen	340	210	110	2.4	4.3	9.0	..	..	7.6	7.6	7.4	0.0	0.2
45	Congo	220	125	108	2.8	1.0	8.7	2.7	-2.9	5.9	6.3	6.1	-0.3	0.2
46	Cameroon	264	173	106	2.1	3.3	8.3	2.4	-6.9	5.8	6.4	5.5	-0.5	1.0
47	Bolivia	252	170	105	2.0	3.2	8.1	1.7	1.7	6.7	5.6	4.6	0.9	1.3
48	Papua New Guinea	248	95	95	4.8	0.0	8.1	..	2.2	6.3	5.7	4.8	0.5	1.1
49	Kenya	202	112	90	2.9	1.5	8.1	3.1	0.0	8.0	7.8	6.0	0.1	1.7
50	Turkmenistan	..	126	85	..	2.6	3.9	..	-1.5	6.4	5.1	3.8	1.1	2.0
51	Tajikistan	..	125	79	..	3.1	5.1	..	-11.4	6.3	5.7	4.7	0.5	1.3
52	Namibia	206	114	78	3.0	2.5	6.7	..	3.3	6.0	5.9	5.1	0.1	1.0
53	Indonesia	216	128	75	2.6	3.5	3.4	5.2	6.0	5.5	4.4	2.8	1.1	3.0
54	Morocco	215	145	75	2.0	4.4	5.6	2.7	1.2	7.2	5.5	3.4	1.3	3.2
55	Mongolia	185	112	74	2.5	2.8	5.4	..	-3.2	6.0	5.4	3.4	0.5	3.1
56	Zimbabwe	181	125	74	1.8	3.5	6.6	1.7	-0.5	7.5	6.4	4.8	0.8	1.9
57	Iraq	171	83	71	3.6	1.0	15.9	..	..	7.2	6.5	5.5	0.5	1.1
58	Guatemala	205	136	67	2.0	4.7	3.4	3.0	0.9	6.9	6.3	5.1	0.5	1.4
59	South Africa	126	91	67	1.6	2.1	6.4	3.2	-1.3	6.5	4.9	4.0	1.4	1.4
60	Libyan Arab Jamahiriya	269	118	63	4.1	4.2	3.9	0.0	..	7.1	7.3	6.2	-0.1	1.1
61	Uzbekistan	..	98	62	..	3.1	3.3	..	-2.3	6.3	4.9	3.7	1.3	1.9
62	Algeria	243	145	61	2.6	5.7	2.9	4.2	-2.5	7.3	6.8	3.6	0.4	4.2
63	Brazil	181	93	60	3.3	2.9	5.3	6.3	-0.4	6.2	3.9	2.8	2.3	2.2
64	Nicaragua	209	143	60	1.9	5.8	3.6	-0.7	-6.1	7.4	6.2	4.8	0.9	1.7
65	Peru	236	130	55	3.0	5.7	2.2	0.8	-2.0	6.9	5.0	3.3	1.6	2.8
66	Kyrgyzstan	..	90	54	..	3.4	4.1	..	-5.0	5.1	4.1	3.5	1.1	1.1
67	Philippines	102	70	53	1.9	1.8	5.0	3.2	1.7	6.9	4.9	3.8	1.7	1.7
68	Botswana	170	94	52	3.0	3.9	4.6	9.9	6.6	6.8	6.1	4.7	0.5	1.7
69	Egypt	258	180	51	1.8	8.4	-0.9	2.8	1.3	7.0	5.2	3.7	1.5	2.3
70	Azerbaijan	..	59	50	..	1.1	9.4	..	-12.2	5.5	3.3	2.4	2.6	2.1
71	Turkey	217	141	50	2.2	6.9	-1.3	3.6	1.4	6.3	4.3	3.2	1.9	2.0
72	China	209	65	47	5.9	2.1	8.1	4.1	7.8	5.5	2.9	2.0	3.2	2.5
73	Kazakstan	..	71	47	..	2.8	3.9	..	-6.5	4.5	3.0	2.4	2.0	1.5
74	Viet Nam	219	105	45	3.7	5.6	4.2	..	..	6.1	5.1	3.7	0.9	2.1
75	Dominican Rep.	152	94	44	2.4	5.0	3.3	3.8	2.2	7.4	4.3	2.9	2.7	2.6

96

		Under-5 mortality rate			average annual rate of reduction (%)			GNP per capita average annual growth rate (%)		Total fertility rate			average annual rate of reduction (%)	
		1960	1980	1995	1960-80	1980-95	required* 1995-2000	1965-80	1985-94	1960	1980	1995	1960-80	1980-95
76	Albania	151	57	40	4.9	2.4	7.7	..	-6.0	5.9	3.8	2.8	2.2	2.0
77	Ecuador	180	101	40	2.9	6.2	3.7	5.4	0.9	6.7	5.1	3.3	1.4	2.9
78	El Salvador	210	120	40	2.8	7.3	2.1	1.5	2.2	6.8	5.4	3.8	1.2	2.3
79	Iran, Islamic Rep. of	233	126	40	3.1	7.6	0.4	2.9	-1.0	7.2	6.7	4.8	0.4	2.2
80	Lebanon	85	40	40	3.8	0.0	8.1	..	..	6.3	4.0	2.9	2.3	2.1
81	Honduras	203	100	38	3.6	6.4	2.2	1.1	0.5	7.5	6.3	4.6	0.9	2.1
82	Tunisia	244	102	37	4.4	6.7	2.1	4.7	2.1	7.1	5.3	3.0	1.5	3.8
83	Colombia	132	59	36	4.1	3.2	7.1	3.7	2.4	6.8	3.8	2.6	2.9	2.5
84	Syrian Arab Rep.	201	73	36	5.1	4.7	4.0	5.1	-2.1	7.3	7.4	5.6	-0.1	1.9
85	Moldova	..	49	34	..	2.4	5.9	..	..	3.3	2.5	2.1	1.4	1.2
86	Paraguay	90	61	34	1.9	3.9	6.4	4.1	1.0	6.8	4.8	4.1	1.7	1.1
87	Saudi Arabia	292	90	34	5.9	6.5	2.5	4.0x	-1.7	7.2	7.3	6.2	-0.1	1.1
88	Mexico	148	87	32	2.7	6.7	4.2	3.6	0.9	6.8	4.7	3.0	1.8	3.0
89	Thailand	146	61	32	4.4	4.2	5.5	4.4	8.6	6.4	3.6	2.1	2.9	3.6
90	Armenia	..	34	31	..	0.6	6.2	..	-13.0	4.5	2.4	2.5	3.1	-0.3
91	TFYR Macedonia	177	69	31	4.7	5.3	2.5	..	..	4.2	2.6	2.0	2.4	1.7
92	Korea, Dem. Peo. Rep.	120	43	30	5.1	2.5	5.1	..	..	5.8	3.1	2.3	3.1	2.0
93	Russian Federation	..	43	30	..	2.4	5.6	..	-4.1	2.6	2.0	1.5	1.3	1.9
94	Romania	82	36	29	4.1	1.4	5.5	..	-4.5	2.3	2.4	1.5	-0.2	3.1
95	Argentina	68	41	27	2.5	2.8	8.2	1.7	2.0	3.1	3.3	2.7	-0.3	1.3
96	Georgia	..	40	26	..	2.9	4.6	..	-18.6	2.9	2.3	2.1	1.2	0.6
97	Latvia	..	36	26	..	2.2	8.1	..	-6.0	1.9	2.0	1.6	-0.3	1.5
98	Jordan	149	66	25	4.1	6.4	1.6	5.8x	-5.6	7.7	7.1	5.4	0.4	1.8
99	Oman	300	95	25	5.7	8.9	1.4	9.0	0.5	7.2	7.2	6.9	0.0	0.3
100	Ukraine	..	31	24	..	1.7	8.1	..	-8.0	2.2	2.0	1.6	0.5	1.5
101	Venezuela	70	42	24	2.6	3.8	6.2	2.3	0.7	6.6	4.2	3.1	2.3	2.0
102	Yugoslavia	120	44	23	5.0	4.3	2.8	..	..	2.7	2.3	2.0	0.8	0.9
103	Mauritius	84	42	23	3.4	4.1	5.7	3.7	5.8	5.8	2.8	2.3	3.6	1.3
104	Estonia	..	30	22	..	2.1	7.3	..	-6.1	2.0	2.1	1.6	-0.2	1.8
105	Uruguay	47	42	21	0.6	4.6	5.8	2.5	2.9	2.9	2.7	2.3	0.4	1.1
106	Belarus	..	32	20	..	3.1	5.4	..	-1.9	2.7	2.1	1.7	1.3	1.4
107	Panama	104	31	20	6.0	2.9	7.3	2.8	-1.2	5.9	3.8	2.8	2.2	2.0
108	Bulgaria	70	25	19	5.1	1.8	9.2	..	-2.7	2.2	2.1	1.5	0.2	2.2
109	Lithuania	..	28	19	..	2.6	7.1	..	-8.0	2.5	2.1	1.8	0.9	1.0
110	Sri Lanka	130	52	19	4.6	6.7	4.3	2.8	2.9	5.3	3.5	2.4	2.1	2.5
111	United Arab Emirates	240	64	19	6.6	8.1	3.4	..	0.4	6.9	5.4	4.1	1.2	1.8
112	Trinidad and Tobago	73	40	18	3.0	5.3	2.2	3.1	-2.3	5.1	3.3	2.3	2.2	2.4
113	Bosnia and Herzegovina	155	38	17	7.0	5.4	4.9	..	..	4.0	2.1	1.6	3.2	1.8
114	Poland	70	24	16	5.3	2.7	6.0	..	0.8	3.0	2.3	1.9	1.3	1.3
115	Costa Rica	112	29	16	6.8	3.8	8.2	3.3	2.8	7.0	3.7	3.0	3.2	1.4
116	Slovakia	..	23	15	..	2.7	8.5	..	-3.0	3.1	2.4	1.9	1.3	1.6
117	Chile	138	35	15	6.9	5.6	2.1	0.0	6.5	5.3	2.8	2.5	3.2	0.8
118	Croatia	98	23	14	7.2	3.1	8.1	..	..	2.3	2.0	1.7	0.7	1.1
119	Hungary	57	26	14	3.9	4.2	4.7	5.1	-1.2	2.0	2.0	1.7	0.0	1.1
120	Kuwait	128	35	14	6.6	6.2	4.4	0.6x	1.1	7.3	5.4	3.0	1.5	3.9
121	Jamaica	76	39	13	3.4	7.2	4.1	-0.1	3.9	5.4	3.8	2.2	1.8	3.6
122	Malaysia	105	42	13	4.6	7.8	-1.0	4.7	5.6	6.8	4.2	3.4	2.4	1.4
123	Portugal	112	31	11	6.4	6.9	0.6	4.6	4.0	3.1	2.2	1.6	1.7	2.1
124	Cuba	50	26	10	3.3	6.0	3.6	..	..	4.2	2.0	1.8	3.7	0.7
125	United States	30	15	10	3.3	2.8	6.3	1.8	1.3	3.5	1.8	2.1	3.3	-1.0
126	Czech Rep.	..	20	10	..	4.8	3.9	..	-2.1	2.3	2.2	1.8	0.2	1.3
127	Belgium	35	15	10	4.3	3.0	8.2	3.6	2.3	2.6	1.6	1.7	2.4	-0.4
128	Greece	64	23	10	5.2	5.8	5.0	4.8	1.3	2.2	2.1	1.4	0.2	2.7
129	Spain	57	16	9	6.2	3.7	7.8	4.1	2.8	2.8	2.2	1.2	1.2	4.0
130	Korea, Rep. of	124	18	9	9.8	4.4	5.3	7.3	7.8	5.7	2.6	1.8	3.9	2.5
131	France	34	13	9	4.9	2.3	7.6	3.7	1.6	2.8	1.9	1.7	1.9	0.7
132	Israel	39	19	9	3.6	5.3	2.2	3.7	2.3	3.9	3.3	2.8	0.8	1.1
133	New Zealand	26	16	9	2.5	4.0	0.7	1.7	0.7	3.9	2.1	2.1	3.1	0.0
134	Slovenia	45	18	8	4.6	5.2	4.0	..	1.2	2.4	2.1	1.5	0.7	2.2
135	Australia	24	13	8	3.0	3.5	4.5	2.2	1.2	3.3	2.0	1.9	2.5	0.3
136	Italy	50	17	8	5.3	5.3	3.6	3.2	1.8	2.5	1.7	1.3	1.9	1.8
137	Netherlands	22	11	8	3.4	2.4	5.8	2.7	1.9	3.1	1.5	1.6	3.6	-0.4
138	Norway	23	11	8	3.8	2.2	3.4	3.6	1.4	2.9	1.8	2.0	2.4	-0.7
139	Canada	33	13	8	4.8	3.6	5.5	3.3	0.3	3.8	1.7	1.9	4.0	-0.7
140	Austria	43	17	7	4.6	5.6	3.2	4.0	2.0	2.7	1.6	1.6	2.6	0.0
141	United Kingdom	27	14	7	3.1	4.3	3.9	2.0	1.3	2.7	1.8	1.8	2.0	0.0
142	Switzerland	27	11	7	4.5	2.7	3.6	1.5	0.5	2.4	1.5	1.6	2.4	-0.4
143	Ireland	36	14	7	4.6	4.6	3.6	2.8	5.0	3.8	3.2	2.1	0.9	2.8
144	Germany	40	16	7	4.7	5.5	3.1	3.0x	1.9	2.4	1.5	1.3	2.4	1.0
145	Denmark	25	10	7	4.4	2.8	2.5	2.2	1.3	2.6	1.6	1.7	2.4	-0.4
146	Japan	40	11	6	6.6	3.5	8.3	5.1	3.2	2.0	1.8	1.5	0.5	1.2
147	Hong Kong*	52	13	6	6.9	5.2	4.1	6.2	5.3	5.0	2.1	1.2	4.3	3.7
148	Singapore	40	13	6	5.6	5.7	0.7	8.3	6.1	5.5	1.8	1.7	5.6	0.4
149	Finland	28	9	5	5.9	3.6	2.5	3.6	-0.3	2.7	1.7	1.9	2.3	-0.7
150	Sweden	20	9	5	4.1	3.9	1.7	2.0	-0.1	2.3	1.6	2.1	1.8	-1.8

*The average annual reduction rate required to achieve an under-five mortality rate in all countries of 70 per 1000 live births or of two thirds the 1990 rate, whichever is the less.
Countries listed in descending order of their 1995 under-five mortality rates (table 1).

Table 10: Regional summaries

	Sub-Saharan Africa	Middle East and North Africa	South Asia	East Asia and Pacific	Latin America and Caribbean	CEE/CIS and Baltic States	Industrialized countries	Developing Countries	Least Developed Countries	World
Table 1: Basic indicators										
Under-5 mortality rate 1960	256	244	238	200	159	..	37	216	283	191
Under-5 mortality rate 1995	175	60	121	55	47	38	8	99	173	90
Infant mortality rate 1960	153	154	146	133	106	..	31	138	172	123
Infant mortality rate 1995	106	46	82	42	38	33	7	67	109	61
Total population (millions)	564	309	1259	1786	474	474	830	4526	586	5696
Annual no. of births (thousands)	24710	10187	38071	35975	11865	7298	10518	124197	24513	138624
Annual no. of under-5 deaths (thousands)	4323	616	4616	1984	554	282	90	12278	4243	12465
GNP per capita (US$)	503	1662	325	962	3139	2121	24300	1023	233	4498
Life expectancy at birth (years)	51	65	61	67	69	69	77	62	52	64
Total adult literacy rate (%)	57	59	49	84	86	96	95	71	49	74
% enrolled in primary school	72	92	91	114	108	97	104	98	66	99
% share of household income, lowest 40%	..	..	21	18	10	18	18	15	..	..
% share of household income, highest 20%	..	..	42	45	61	45	41	51	..	..
Table 2: Nutrition										
% with low birth weight	16	11	33	11	10	..	6	19	23	18
% of children who are exclusively breastfed, 0-3 months	29	43	46	..	21	..	..	42	43	42
% of children who are breastfed with food, 6-9 months	64	45	31	..	41	..	..	45	53	45
% of children who are still breastfeeding, 20-23 months	48	..	68	..	20	..	..	52	57	52
% of children suffering from underweight, moderate & severe	30	16	52	23	11	..	..	32	42	32
% of children suffering from underweight, severe	9	4	20	4	2	..	..	10	14	10
% of children suffering from wasting, moderate & severe	8	7	16	5	3	..	..	9	10	9
% of children suffering from stunting, moderate & severe	41	24	53	34	20	..	..	39	50	39
Total goitre rate (%)	16	20	13	13	15	20	..	15	19	14
% of households consuming iodized salt	47	75	58	48	80	26	..	55	33	54
Calorie supply as % of requirements	93	123	99	112	114	128	134	107	90	112
Table 3: Health										
% with access to safe water, total	51	79	80	67	75	..	..	71	55	71
% with access to safe water, urban	80	95	85	93	86	..	..	88	77	89
% with access to safe water, rural	36	59	78	57	55	..	..	61	48	61
% with access to adequate sanitation, total	44	60	33	35	61	..	..	40	35	40
% with access to adequate sanitation, urban	73	86	71	76	71	..	..	74	63	75
% with access to adequate sanitation, rural	32	44	19	18	32	..	..	22	27	22
% with access to health services, total	53	87	77	87	79	..	..	80	40	80
% with access to health services, urban	80	99	..	..	..	..	..	..	..	97
% with access to health services, rural	..	79	..	..	..	..	..	..	..	76
% of 1-year-olds immunized against TB	68	95	90	91	96	82	..	87	73	87
% of 1-year-olds immunized against DPT	51	88	77	89	84	83	86	77	58	78
% of 1-year-olds immunized against polio	50	88	84	90	84	84	88	80	58	81
% of 1-year-olds immunized against measles	53	86	73	88	85	80	83	76	59	77
% of pregnant women immunized against tetanus	39	62	69	35	53	..	..	50	49	50
ORT use rate (%)	73	51	48	87	64	..	..	65	81	65
Table 4: Education										
Adult literacy rate 1980, male (%)	51	55	52	81	82	..	..	69	47	74
Adult literacy rate 1980, female (%)	30	27	24	58	78	..	..	46	24	56
Adult literacy rate 1995, male (%)	67	70	63	91	88	98	..	79	59	81
Adult literacy rate 1995, female (%)	48	47	36	76	85	94	..	62	38	66
No. of radio sets per 1000 population	148	252	79	197	346	392	1255	177	96	355
No. of television sets per 1000 population	24	98	33	49	164	313	594	59	10	157
Primary school enrolment ratio (%) 1960 (gross), male	47	67	77	120	75	..	109	93	47	95
Primary school enrolment ratio (%) 1960 (gross), female	24	35	39	85	71	..	109	62	23	68
Primary school enrolment ratio (%) 1990-94 (gross), male	80	99	102	116	106	98	104	103	74	103
Primary school enrolment ratio (%) 1990-94 (gross), female	66	84	80	112	103	96	104	92	59	93
Primary school enrolment ratio (%) 1990-95 (net), male	58	92	..	97	86	..	97	86	56	88
Primary school enrolment ratio (%) 1990-95 (net), female	50	82	..	95	86	..	97	81	45	84
% reaching grade 5, primary school	71	91	59	87	73	94	99	75	57	76
Secondary school enrolment ratio, male (%)	26	62	51	57	45	80	97	51	21	57
Secondary school enrolment ratio, female (%)	21	49	32	49	49	82	99	41	12	49

	Sub-Saharan Africa	Middle East and North Africa	South Asia	East Asia and Pacific	Latin America and Caribbean	CEE/CIS and Baltic States	Industrialized countries	Developing Countries	Least Developed Countries	World
Table 5: Demographic indicators										
Population under 18 (millions)	293	148	539	603	190	141	191	1827	294	2106
Population under 5 (millions)	103	46	168	171	56	36	53	560	101	633
Population annual growth rate 1965-80 (%)	2.7	2.9	2.3	2.2	2.5	1.1	0.8	2.3	2.5	2.0
Population annual growth rate 1980-95 (%)	2.9	3.0	2.2	1.5	2.0	0.8	0.6	2.0	2.6	1.7
Crude death rate 1960	24	21	21	19	13	10	10	20	25	17
Crude death rate 1995	15	7	9	7	6	11	9	9	14	9
Crude birth rate 1960	49	48	44	39	42	25	20	42	48	36
Crude birth rate 1995	44	33	30	20	25	15	13	28	42	24
Life expectancy 1960 (years)	40	47	44	48	56	65	70	47	39	51
Life expectancy 1995 (years)	51	65	61	67	69	69	77	62	52	64
Total fertility rate	6.1	4.6	3.9	2.3	3.0	2.1	1.7	3.4	5.6	3.1
% of population urbanized	31	54	27	33	74	66	77	37	22	45
Urban population annual growth rate 1965-80 (%)	5.2	4.8	3.8	3.3	3.8	2.3	1.3	3.8	5.4	2.8
Urban population annual growth rate 1980-95 (%)	5.0	4.1	3.4	4.1	2.9	1.8	0.8	3.8	5.0	2.8
Table 6: Economic indicators										
GNP per capita (US$)	503	1662	325	962	3139	2121	24300	1023	233	4498
GNP per capita annual growth rate 1965-80 (%)	2.7	3.1	1.5	4.9	4.0	. .	2.9	3.7	-0.1	3.1
GNP per capita annual growth rate 1985-94 (%)	-0.9	-0.7	2.6	7.1	0.9	-3.1	1.9	2.9	-0.1	1.9
Annual rate of inflation (%)	16	15	10	9	392	103	3	139	22	30
% below absolute poverty level, urban	. .	. .	33	. .	18	. .	. .	27	55	. .
% below absolute poverty level, rural	62	. .	39	16	48	. .	. .	31	70	. .
% of government expenditure to health	4	6	2	2	5	. .	12	4	5	10
% of government expenditure to education	13	15	3	12	10	. .	4	11	12	6
% of government expenditure to defence	11	21	17	17	5	. .	10	13	19	10
ODA inflow (US$ millions)	17285	6296	7035	8637	5112	. .	. .	45138	15676	48299
ODA inflow as % of recipient GNP	6	1	2	1	0	. .	. .	1	12	1
Debt service, % of goods & services exports 1970	6	12	17	6	13	. .	. .	11	6	11
Debt service, % of goods & services exports 1994	85	383	291	367	205	2109	. .	254	53	286
Table 7: Women										
Life expectancy, females as % of males	106	104	101	106	108	112	109	104	104	105
Adult literacy, females as % of males	71	67	57	84	97	96	. .	78	63	81
Enrolment, females as % of males, primary school	83	85	79	97	97	98	100	89	79	90
Enrolment, females as % of males, secondary school	80	79	63	87	109	102	101	81	59	87
Contraceptive prevalence (%)	15	44	38	75	60	. .	72	54	18	57
Pregnant women immunized against tetanus (%)	39	62	69	35	53	. .	. .	50	49	50
% of births attended by trained health personnel	38	62	29	75	76	. .	99	53	29	57
Maternal mortality rate	980	323	607	214	190	88	13	477	1052	428
Table 9: The rate of progress										
Under-5 mortality rate 1960	256	244	238	200	159	. .	37	216	283	191
Under-5 mortality rate 1980	202	142	179	81	88	63	15	137	221	122
Under-5 mortality rate 1995	175	60	121	55	47	38	8	99	173	90
Under-5 mortality annual reduction rate 1960-80 (%)	1.2	2.7	1.4	4.5	3.0	. .	4.7	2.3	1.2	2.2
Under-5 mortality annual reduction rate 1980-95 (%)	1.0	5.7	2.6	2.5	4.2	3.3	3.6	2.2	1.6	2.1
Under-5 mortality annual reduction rate required 1995-2000 (%)	18.9	5.0	11.1	7.6	5.1	3.3	5.7	11.8	18.1	11.6
GNP per capita annual growth rate 1965-80 (%)	2.7	3.1	1.5	4.9	4.0	. .	2.9	3.7	-0.1	3.1
GNP per capita annual growth rate 1985-94 (%)	-0.9	-0.7	2.6	7.1	0.9	-3.1	1.9	2.9	-0.1	1.9
Total fertility rate 1960	6.6	7.1	6.1	5.6	6.0	3.0	2.8	6.0	6.6	4.9
Total fertility rate 1980	6.6	6.2	5.1	3.3	4.1	2.5	1.8	4.4	6.5	3.8
Total fertility rate 1995	6.1	4.6	3.9	2.3	3.0	2.1	1.7	3.4	5.6	3.1
Total fertility annual reduction rate 1960-80 (%)	0.0	0.7	0.9	2.7	1.8	0.9	2.2	1.5	0.0	1.3
Total fertility annual reduction rate 1980-95 (%)	0.6	2.0	1.7	2.4	2.2	1.4	0.2	1.7	1.0	1.4

Figures in this table are totals or weighted averages.

Country groupings for table 10

Sub-Saharan Africa	Angola	Eritrea	Madagascar	Senegal
	Benin	Ethiopia	Malawi	Sierra Leone
	Botswana	Gabon	Mali	Somalia
	Burkina Faso	Gambia	Mauritania	South Africa
	Burundi	Ghana	Mauritius	Tanzania , U. Rep. of
	Cameroon	Guinea	Mozambique	Togo
	Central African Rep.	Guinea-Bissau	Namibia	Uganda
	Chad	Kenya	Niger	Zaire
	Congo	Lesotho	Nigeria	Zambia
	Côte d'Ivoire	Liberia	Rwanda	Zimbabwe

Middle East and North Africa	Algeria	Jordan	Morocco	Syrian Arab Rep.
	Egypt	Kuwait	Oman	Tunisia
	Iran, Islamic Rep. of	Lebanon	Saudi Arabia	United Arab Emirates
	Iraq	Libyan Arab Jamahiriya	Sudan	Yemen

South Asia	Afghanistan	Bhutan	Nepal	Sri Lanka
	Bangladesh	India	Pakistan	

East Asia and Pacific	Cambodia	Korea, Dem. Peo. Rep.	Mongolia	Singapore
	China	Korea, Rep. of	Myanmar	Thailand
	Hong Kong*	Lao Peo. Dem. Rep.	Papua New Guinea	Viet Nam
	Indonesia	Malaysia	Philippines	

Latin America and Caribbean	Argentina	Cuba	Honduras	Peru
	Bolivia	Dominican Rep.	Jamaica	Trinidad and Tobago
	Brazil	Ecuador	Mexico	Uruguay
	Chile	El Salvador	Nicaragua	Venezuela
	Colombia	Guatemala	Panama	
	Costa Rica	Haiti	Paraguay	

Central and Eastern Europe, Commonwealth of Independent States, and Baltic States	Albania	Czech Rep.	Moldova	Turkmenistan
	Armenia	Estonia	Poland	Ukraine
	Azerbaijan	Georgia	Romania	Uzbekistan
	Belarus	Hungary	Russian Federation	Yugoslavia
	Bosnia and	Kazakstan	Slovakia	
	Herzegovina	Kyrgyzstan	Tajikistan	
	Bulgaria	Latvia	TFYR Macedonia	
	Croatia	Lithuania	Turkey	

Industrialized countries	Australia	France	Japan	Spain
	Austria	Germany	Netherlands	Sweden
	Belgium	Greece	New Zealand	Switzerland
	Canada	Ireland	Norway	United Kingdom
	Denmark	Israel	Portugal	United States
	Finland	Italy	Slovenia	

Developing countries	Afghanistan	El Salvador	Liberia	Senegal
	Algeria	Eritrea	Libyan Arab	Sierra Leone
	Angola	Ethiopia	Jamahiriya	Singapore
	Argentina	Gabon	Madagascar	Somalia
	Armenia	Gambia	Malawi	South Africa
	Azerbaijan	Georgia	Malaysia	Sri Lanka
	Bangladesh	Ghana	Mali	Sudan
	Benin	Guatemala	Mauritania	Syrian Arab Rep.
	Bhutan	Guinea	Mauritius	Tajikistan
	Bolivia	Guinea-Bissau	Mexico	Tanzania , U. Rep. of
	Botswana	Haiti	Mongolia	Thailand
	Brazil	Honduras	Morocco	Togo
	Burkina Faso	Hong Kong*	Mozambique	Trinidad and Tobago
	Burundi	India	Myanmar	Tunisia
	Cambodia	Indonesia	Namibia	Turkey
	Cameroon	Iran, Islamic Rep. of	Nepal	Turkmenistan
	Central African Rep.	Iraq	Nicaragua	Uganda
	Chad	Jamaica	Niger	United Arab Emirates
	Chile	Jordan	Nigeria	Uruguay
	China	Kazakstan	Oman	Uzbekistan
	Colombia	Kenya	Pakistan	Venezuela
	Congo	Korea, Dem. Peo. Rep.	Panama	Viet Nam
	Costa Rica	Korea, Rep. of	Papua New Guinea	Yemen
	Côte d'Ivoire	Kuwait	Paraguay	Zaire
	Cuba	Kyrgyzstan	Peru	Zambia
	Dominican Rep.	Lao Peo. Dem. Rep.	Philippines	Zimbabwe
	Ecuador	Lebanon	Rwanda	
	Egypt	Lesotho	Saudi Arabia	

Least developed countries	Afghanistan	Eritrea	Malawi	Sudan
	Angola	Ethiopia	Mali	Tanzania , U. Rep. of
	Bangladesh	Gambia	Mauritania	Togo
	Benin	Guinea	Mozambique	Uganda
	Bhutan	Guinea-Bissau	Myanmar	Yemen
	Burkina Faso	Haiti	Nepal	Zaire
	Burundi	Lao Peo. Dem. Rep.	Niger	Zambia
	Cambodia	Lesotho	Rwanda	
	Central African Rep.	Liberia	Sierra Leone	
	Chad	Madagascar	Somalia	

Definitions

Under-five mortality rate
Probability of dying between birth and exactly five years of age expressed per 1,000 live births.

Infant mortality rate
Probability of dying between birth and exactly one year of age expressed per 1,000 live births.

GNP
Gross national product, expressed in current United States dollars. GNP per capita growth rates are average annual growth rates that have been computed by fitting trend lines to the logarithmic values of GNP per capita at constant market prices for each year of the time period.

Life expectancy at birth
The number of years newborn children would live if subject to the mortality risks prevailing for the cross-section of population at the time of their birth.

Adult literacy rate
Percentage of persons aged 15 and over who can read and write.

Primary and secondary enrolment ratios
The gross enrolment ratio is the total number of children enrolled in a schooling level — whether or not they belong in the relevant age group for that level — expressed as a percentage of the total number of children in the relevant age group for that level. The net enrolment ratio is the total number of children enrolled in a schooling level who belong in the relevant age group, expressed as a percentage of the total number in that age group.

Income share
Percentage of income received by the 20 per cent of households with the highest income and by the 40 per cent of households with the lowest income.

Low birth weight
Less than 2,500 grams.

Underweight
Moderate and severe – below minus two standard deviations from median weight for age of reference population; severe — below minus three standard deviations from median weight for age of reference population.

Wasting
Moderate and severe – below minus two standard deviations from median weight for height of reference population.

Stunting
Moderate and severe – below minus two standard deviations from median height for age of reference population.

Total goitre rate
Percentage of children aged 6-11 with palpable or visible goitre. This is an indicator of iodine deficiency, which causes brain damage and mental retardation.

Access to health services
Percentage of the population that can reach appropriate local health services by the local means of transport in no more than one hour.

DPT
Diphtheria, pertussis (whooping cough) and tetanus.

ORT use
Percentage of all cases of diarrhoea in children under five years of age treated with oral rehydration salts or recommended home fluids.

Children reaching grade 5 of primary school
Percentage of the children entering the first grade of primary school who eventually reach grade 5.

Crude death rate
Annual number of deaths per 1,000 population.

Crude birth rate
Annual number of births per 1,000 population.

Total fertility rate
The number of children that would be born per woman if she were to live to the end of her child-bearing years and bear children at each age in accordance with prevailing age-specific fertility rates.

Urban population
Percentage of population living in urban areas as defined according to the national definition used in the most recent population census.

Absolute poverty level
The income level below which a minimum nutritionally adequate diet plus essential non-food requirements is not affordable.

ODA
Official development assistance.

Debt service
The sum of interest payments and repayments of principal on external public and publicly guaranteed long-term debts.

Contraceptive prevalence
Percentage of married women aged 15-49 years currently using contraception.

Births attended
Percentage of births attended by physicians, nurses, midwives, or primary health care workers trained in midwifery skills.

Maternal mortality rate
Annual number of deaths of women from pregnancy-related causes per 100,000 live births.

Main sources

Under-five and infant mortality
United Nations Population Division, UNICEF, United Nations Statistical Division, World Bank and US Bureau of the Census.

Total population
United Nations Population Division.

Births
United Nations Population Division, United Nations Statistical Division and World Bank.

Under-five deaths
UNICEF.

GNP per capita
World Bank.

Life expectancy
United Nations Population Division.

Adult literacy
United Nations Educational, Scientific and Cultural Organization (UNESCO).

School enrolment and reaching grade 5
United Nations Educational, Scientific and Cultural Organization (UNESCO).

Household income
World Bank.

Low birth weight
World Health Organization (WHO).

Breastfeeding
Demographic and Health Surveys (Macro International), Multiple Indicator Cluster Surveys (MICS) and World Health Organization (WHO).

Underweight, wasting and stunting
Demographic and Health Surveys, Multiple Indicator Cluster Surveys (MICS) and World Health Organization (WHO).

Salt iodization
UNICEF and Multiple Indicator Cluster Surveys (MICS).

Goitre rate
World Health Organization (WHO).

Calorie intake
Food and Agricultural Organization of the United Nations (FAO).

Access to safe drinking water and adequate sanitation facilities
UNICEF, World Health Organization (WHO) and Multiple Indicator Cluster Surveys (MICS).

Access to health services
UNICEF and Demographic and Health Surveys.

Immunization
World Health Organization (WHO) and UNICEF.

ORT use
Multiple Indicator Cluster Surveys (MICS), Demographic and Health Surveys and World Health Organization (WHO).

Radio and television
United Nations Educational, Scientific and Cultural Organization (UNESCO).

Child population
United Nations Population Division.

Crude death and birth rates
United Nations Population Division.

Fertility
United Nations Population Division.

Urban population
United Nations Population Division and World Bank

Inflation and absolute poverty level
World Bank.

Expenditure on health, education and defense
International Monetary Fund (IMF).

ODA
Organisation for Economic Co-operation and Development (OECD).

Debt service
World Bank.

Contraceptive prevalence
United Nations Population Division and Demographic and Health Surveys.

Births attended
World Health Organization (WHO).

Maternal mortality
World Health Organization (WHO) and UNICEF.
Several of the maternal mortality rates in table 7 are substantially different from official government estimates. These and other rates are being reviewed by WHO and UNICEF and will be revised where necessary, as part of the ongoing process of improving maternal mortality estimates.

Index

Glossary

AIDS
acquired immune deficiency syndrome

BGMEA
Bangladesh Garment Manufacturers and Exporters Association

BGUS
Balia Gram Unnayan Samity project

BRAC
Bangladesh Rural Advancement Committee

CEE/CIS
Central and Eastern Europe/Commonwealth of Independent States

CLASS
Child Labour Abolition Support Scheme

CREDA
Centre for Rural Education and Development Association

EN
Escuela Nueva

ENDA-Tiers Monde
Environment and Development Action in the Third World

GNP
gross national product

GTZ
German Agency for Technical Cooperation

HIV
human immunodeficiency virus

ICCR
Interfaith Center on Corporate Responsibility

ICFTU
International Confederation of Free Trade Unions

ILO
International Labour Organization

IMF
International Monetary Fund

IPEC
International Programme on the Elimination of Child Labour (ILO)

NGO
non-governmental organization

ODA
official development assistance

OECD
Organisation for Economic Co-operation and Development

ROAD
Rural Organization and Assistance for Development

SAARC
South Asian Association for Regional Cooperation

SACCS
South Asian Coalition on Child Servitude

UN
United Nations

UNDP
United Nations Development Programme

UNESCO
United Nations Educational, Scientific and Cultural Organization

UNICEF
United Nations Children's Fund

ZINTEC
Zimbabwe Integrated National Teacher Education Course

UNICEF Headquarters
3 UN Plaza
New York, NY 10017, USA

UNICEF Geneva Office
Palais des Nations
CH-1211 Geneva 10, Switzerland

UNICEF Regional Office for
Central and Eastern Europe,
Commonwealth of Independent States,
and Baltic States
Palais des Nations
CH-1211 Geneva 10, Switzerland

UNICEF Regional Office for
Eastern and Southern Africa
P.O. Box 44145
Nairobi, Kenya

UNICEF Regional Office for
West and Central Africa
P.O. Box 443
Abidjan 04, Côte d'Ivoire

UNICEF Regional Office for the
Americas and the Caribbean
Apartado 7555
Santa Fe de Bogotá, Colombia

UNICEF Regional Office for
East Asia and the Pacific
P.O. Box 2–154
Bangkok 10200, Thailand

UNICEF Regional Office for the
Middle East and North Africa
P.O. Box 811721
11181 Amman, Jordan

UNICEF Regional Office
for South Asia
P.O. Box 5815
Lekhnath Marg
Kathmandu, Nepal

UNICEF Office for Japan
UN Headquarters Building
8th floor
53-70, Jingumae 5-chome
Shibuya-ku
Tokyo 150, Japan